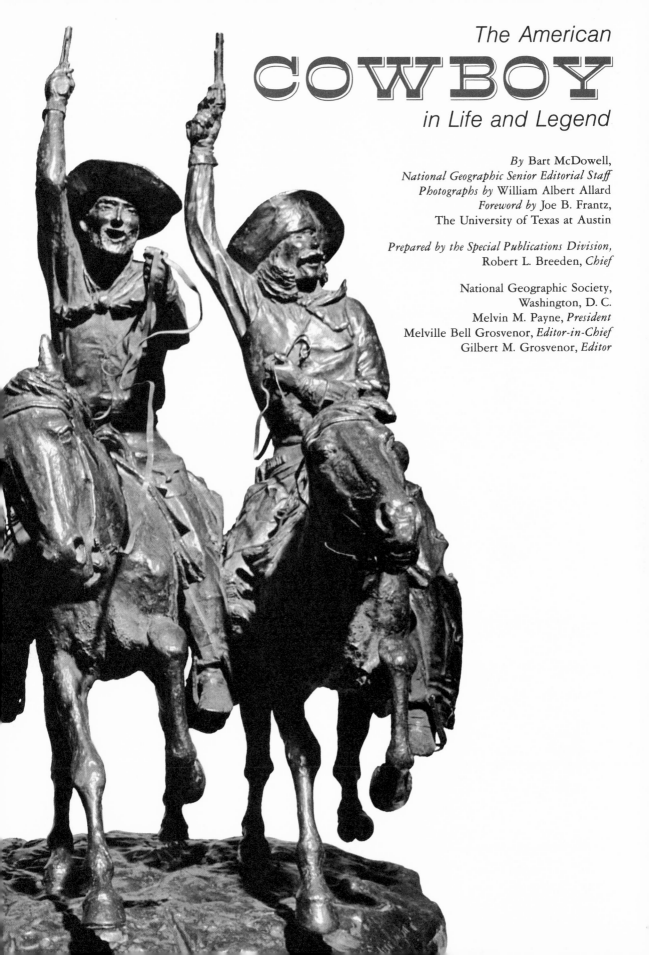

The American COWBOY in Life and Legend

By Bart McDowell,
National Geographic Senior Editorial Staff
Photographs by William Albert Allard
Foreword by Joe B. Frantz,
The University of Texas at Austin

Prepared by the Special Publications Division,
Robert L. Breeden, *Chief*

National Geographic Society,
Washington, D. C.
Melvin M. Payne, *President*
Melville Bell Grosvenor, *Editor-in-Chief*
Gilbert M. Grosvenor, *Editor*

THE AMERICAN COWBOY
IN LIFE AND LEGEND

By BART McDOWELL
National Geographic Senior Editorial Staff
Photographs by WILLIAM ALBERT ALLARD

Published by
THE NATIONAL GEOGRAPHIC SOCIETY
MELVIN M. PAYNE, *President*
MELVILLE BELL GROSVENOR, *Editor-in-Chief*
GILBERT M. GROSVENOR, *Editor*
ROBERT PAUL JORDAN, *Consulting Editor*

Prepared by
THE SPECIAL PUBLICATIONS DIVISION
ROBERT L. BREEDEN, *Editor*
DONALD J. CRUMP, *Associate Editor*
PHILIP B. SILCOTT, *Senior Assistant Editor*
JOHANNA G. FARREN, *Research*

Illustrations
DAVID R. BRIDGE, *Picture Editor*
WILLIAM L. ALLEN, MARGERY G. DUNN,
   WILLIAM R. GRAY, JR., STRATFORD C.
   JONES, H. ROBERT MORRISON, *Picture
   Legends*
TUCKER L. ETHERINGTON, *Picture Legend
   Research*

Layout and Design
JOSEPH A. TANEY, *Art Director*
JOSEPHINE B. BOLT, *Associate Art Director*
URSULA PERRIN, *Design Assistant*
VIRGINIA L. BAZA, BETTY CLONINGER,
   JOHN D. GARST, JR., *Map Research*

Production and Printing
ROBERT W. MESSER, *Production Manager*
MARGARET MURIN SKEKEL, *Production
   Assistant*
JAMES R. WHITNEY, JOHN R. METCALFE,
   Engraving and Printing
MARTA I. BERNAL, SUZANNE J. JACOBSON,
   ELIZABETH VAN BEUREN JOY, RAJA D.
   MURSHED, JOAN PERRY, *Staff Assistants*
DOROTHY M. CORSON, JOLENE McCOY, *Index*

Standard Book Number 87044-099-3
Library of Congress Catalog Card Number 71-151947

*Overleaf: Shots, yells, and pounding hoofs herald
reveling cowboys. Page 1: In the light of a campfire,
a Texas night herder rolls a cigarette. Front Endpaper: A trail hand follows his herd through a
draw on a 1908 drive in Texas. Bookbinding: An
old-time cowman shakes out a loop of rope.*

OVERLEAF: "COMING THROUGH THE RYE," BY FREDERIC REMINGTON,
1902, CORCORAN GALLERY OF ART, WASHINGTON, D. C.; PAGE 1 AND FRONT
ENDPAPER: LIBRARY OF CONGRESS, ERWIN E. SMITH COLLECTION, BOTH
1908; BOOKBINDING AND ART ON CHAPTER TITLE PAGES AFTER CHARLES
M. RUSSELL, FROM THE BOOK "GOOD MEDICINE" BY CHARLES M. RUSSELL,
COPYRIGHT 1929, 1930 BY NANCY C. RUSSELL, PUBLISHED BY
DOUBLEDAY & COMPANY, INC.

*Head buckaroo—foreman—of the
Nevada Garvey Ranch, Brian Morris
rests on his saddle horn during a
rainy autumn cattle drive. He follows
a way of life that reached its heyday
in the decades just after the Civil
War when men who "knew cow"
made their living from the saddle.*

Foreword

WE HUNKERED on our heels, four citified *yanquis* on vacation in Mexico, listening to the velvet twilight voices of the Coahuila *vaqueros* as they cooled their coffee before yielding to the night. The talk was of smart horses, fractious cows, beautiful *señoritas,* good food and drink, and mean weather. Almost invariably the talker was his own hero, as he triumphed again and again.

At last one of us broke our own attentive silence. "I wonder," he mused, "if we could possibly say or do anything that would impress these fellows?"

His was a valid question. Each of us was fairly successful in his own right, but what personal achievement could we discuss that would raise our stature in the eyes of these sombreroed cowboys? Wealth? They lived well on their $50 a month and keep. Political honors? What politician could ride or rope as well as they? Business success, a prize-winning book, a courtroom triumph, a starring role in a movie?

No, we decided, none of the ordinary ambitions and occasional honors mattered here. Whatever exploit we recounted, only innate courtesy would have held their attention. Then they would have turned the conversation back to the old steer that wouldn't come out of the brush, and tell how José or Lorenzo had outsmarted that *ladino* after a real game of wits. Nothing could match stories of determined men on horseback defeating four-legged stubbornness.

For the cowboy lives in a world apart — and has since the first herdsman climbed astride a horse, waved his hat, let out a yell, and chased down a stray. His horse has raised him above the earthbound creatures who walk, and he knows it.

The cowboy knows too that to the world he is the American tradition, whether we are talking of cowboys in Montana, buckaroos in Nevada, or vaqueros in Mexico. He is the one American folk hero — of all the Americas. But he didn't originate here, for the mounted herdsman goes back to Biblical days. Nonetheless, it was in this hemisphere that cowboys became fabled. Writers of penny dreadfuls and other exaggerated fiction portrayed them as modern knights bent on conquering the wilderness and rescuing good from the clutches of evil — and a world seeking heroes gave them instant and enduring status.

And then came Hollywood, with its own group of investors and opportunity seekers. They too perceived the possibilities inherent in the man on horseback. Before long, the cowboy became known and loved in every community with a projector and a screen. Nowadays the American cowboy of legend is so well recognized as a folk hero that his story is retold by film makers in such seemingly unlikely places as Italy, India, and Japan.

But when stripped of all the pretenses of film and fiction, what was the cowboy really like? What is he like now? Author Bart McDowell, who glimpsed the disappearing old-time cowboy on the rough Mexican ranches of his childhood, set out to refresh his memory and to discover what the decades had done to his and our hero. He wanted to remove the cowboy's veneer of glamor, to look at him as a very special workman, special to himself and to all of us. Bart has admirably accomplished what he set out to do; in the process the cowboy emerges again as a man of appeal and, in his own way, a man for all ages.

JOE B. FRANTZ
Professor of History, University of Texas at Austin

Contents

"When Things Are Quiet": A Montana cowboy wearing angora chaps lazes on a hillside overlooking his grazing herd.

PAINTING BY PHILIP R. GOODWIN, 1910, COLLECTION OF NATIONAL COWBOY HALL OF FAME, OKLAHOMA CITY;
CHAPTER TITLES ADAPTED FROM THE LETTERS OF COWBOY-ARTIST CHARLES M. RUSSELL

1

The Weather Worn Cow Men

THE FIRST COWBOY I EVER MET was my own grandfather. By then, of course, his fires were banked. Folks in Del Rio, Texas, all respectfully called him Judge, though he had long retired from both the saddle and the bench.

But even as a small boy I knew that the world was better supplied with judges than with cowboys. Whenever I spent the night at his house, I got him to tell me about "when you were a real cowboy." And so my bedtime stories had more of bear grease than of Goldilocks. Grandfather taught me to sing some rousing Indian songs. He introduced me to my first chili peppers and to chuckwagon treats like son-of-a-gun stew—an alias reserved for my young ears.

Later when my father and grandfather jointly bought a ranch in northern Mexico, I listened to more cowboy tales, told with that special magic that the flames of campfires and kerosene lamps can conjure. I would *(Continued on page 25)*

In drenching rain, ranch hand Res Clute rides out to tend cattle in Wyoming's mountainous Gros Ventre country. A cowboy's life means long, often grueling days broken only rarely by such strenuous excitement as rope work.

"AN OLD TIME COW DOG": BACKHAND TOSS ROPES A LONGHORN.

Hazed by a Nevada buckaroo, a herd evokes the great trail drives of the 19th century

when millions of Longhorns walked out of Texas to railheads and ranges farther north.

Pounding hoofs fling up dust as a cowboy cuts a steer from a herd during a roundup in 1886 near the Powder River, Montana Territory. Star performer at the roundup, a well-trained cutting horse unerringly followed every twist and turn of the animal picked out by the rider. In the days of open range, ranchers joined forces for the spring roundup. Each morning men searched out the cattle; in the afternoon, ranch reps—representatives —gathered them into separate herds, marked calves with the mother's brand, and apportioned mavericks, or unbranded cattle. After dark, the men eased into their bed-rolls near the chuckwagon, leaving the herd in the care of night riders. After a two-hour shift, each rider woke his relief. Pulling off his boots (left), a weary hand settles in.

Getting all slicked up, perhaps for a wild night on the nearest town, cowboys of the 1890's

scrub off accumulated grime. Shaded by wide-brimmed hats, their brows remain untanned.

"Cattle king of America," New Mexico rancher John Chisum stands for a portrait taken in the late 1800's. At one time some 60,000 cattle bore his Long Rail brand—a straight line running from rump to shoulder—and his "jinglebob" earmark—a split that left the bottom half of the ear loose and dangling.

Bill Pickett, turn-of-the-century rodeo star, also ranked as "the greatest sweat and dirt cowhand that ever lived —bar none," in the words of his boss, rancher and showman Zack Miller. Though few rose to fame as Pickett did, black cowboys by the thousand followed the trails of the Old West.

"Grand old man of the Pitchfork," D. B. Gardner (above, center) visits with friends during a 1926 reunion in Fort Worth. The Texas ranch he helped establish in 1883 remains in operation today. Calamity Jane (below, left) often dressed as a man. In 1875 she drove mule trains for the Army—until an officer surprised her taking a swim and fired her on the spot. Cattleman Charles Goodnight (below, right) blazed a stock trail northward out of Texas in 1866.

PAINTING BY WILLIAM HERBERT DUNTON, 1910, THE ROCKWELL FOUNDATION, CORNING, NEW YORK

Raising a racket with the dinner gong, cook Kaye Tapp of the Snake River Ranch calls in the hands for the noon meal. During summer haying, the ranch employs up to 25 men. At far right, a Montana woman picks up the mail after a horseback ride across snowy fields.

"The Helping Hand": Bonneted and gloved, a woman rides herd on dusty Longhorns. Wives and daughters of cattlemen faced a daily struggle for survival with courage and fortitude. "Words are inadequate to express the admiration and respect the cowboys had for those old time ranch women," recalled one man of his years on the Southwestern frontier. Most agreed, and the mere presence of a young lady could reduce the wild cowboy to shy stammering.

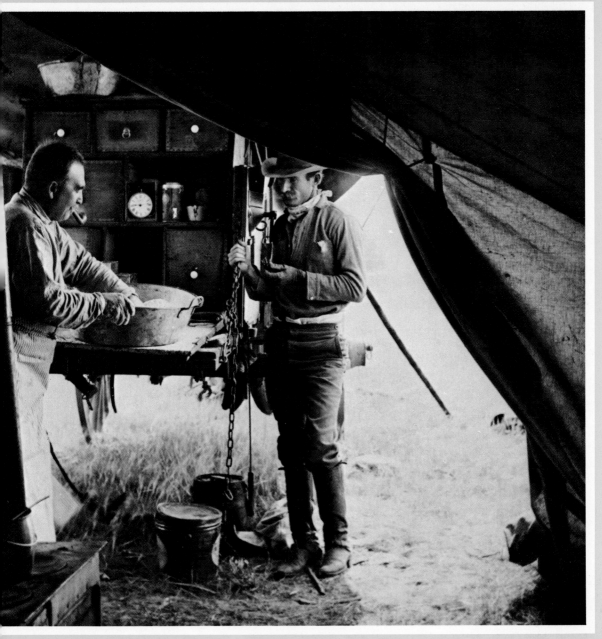

Kneading dough in a dishpan, the cook of the LU Bar Ranch, Montana, makes sourdough bread at the chuck-wagon during a roundup about 1904. Charles Good-night invented the mule-drawn kitchen in 1866 when he nailed a stout cupboard—the chuck box—onto the back of a wagon reinforced to withstand rough trails. A few of the outdoor kitchens remain in use today. On the Pitchfork Ranch near Dickens, Texas, cook Richard J. Bolt (opposite, lower) takes a break while his helper cuts out a pan of sourdough biscuits (opposite, upper).

Men as unlike as the hats they wear share a common trait: love for their calling. Top row, left to right: Theodore "Shorty" Gaulin works as an irrigator for the Snake River Ranch, Jackson, Wyoming. On the Nevada Garvey Ranch, Paradise Valley, buckaroo Stub Stanford lingers at dawn over a last cup of coffee. Cowboy Ron Willis trots Lucky across a sagebrush flat on the Snake River Ranch, and a horse trainer in Mexico

watches his animals in action. Bottom row, left to right: Crew boss Orval Roulston rides for the Douglas Lake Cattle Company in British Columbia, Canada. Jimmie Sherwood wrangles movie horses for Hollywood studios. Foreman Roy Evans supervises the crew of the Snake River Ranch. Pitchfork hand Benny Butler rests after a day in the saddle, and former rodeo star Bob Askin cuts the dust in his throat at Miles City, Montana.

start Grandfather off with a question, and he would respond, "The time I ran away from home? *Which* time? Oh, the time I went to Childress." And off he'd be, at age 18 again, arriving in that Texas town (population about 600 then) in the middle of the night, waking up the desk clerk in "a hotel that looked like a packing crate."

"Don't you want my name?" young Caswell McDowell asked the clerk.

"Son, we don't pay no mind to names here," the clerk replied. "Every other man you meet ain't usin' his real name nohow."

So, without registering, young Cas retired to a squeaky bed and sleep. "I woke up late next morning, sun already out. Jumped up—I still remember putting my bare feet on that raw lumber floor. I walked out on the balcony and I looked out for miles and saw two big herds of antelope grazing right there. Couple of hundred in each herd.

"I just liked the looks of that country. Young, you know. Everything seemed to be wild. So I decided to be wild myself."

At least he tried. For a couple of winter months, he moved into a dugout with his older brother Charlie, homesteading on Section 40. "The dugout was a squat mud-and-lumber contraption with its rump end pushed into the side of a little canyon," he recalled. "In winter it was warmer than any old frame house." He would draw upon his pipe and fill the air with strata of Prince Albert smoke.

"But one trouble was that animals would come stand on the roof. Javelinas and coyotes—I'd never heard coyotes yip before that. And then one morning early when I got up to milk the cows, I found an old black bear standing up on his haunches and batting at the chimney smoke with one paw. He took off fast, but I went after him on the pony, got between him and the brush, and shot him in the head. Well, that night while we were eating bear meat, I got to wondering about Charlie's dugout. Figured it wasn't near wild enough for me, so I lit out west for the Shoe Nail Ranch, and my first job cowpunchin'.

"I got $30 a month and grub. Furnished my own rig and bedroll, of course. The outfit gave each man a mount of ten to a dozen horses.

"Well, I grew my hair long and tried to act mysterious—you know, tried to be in fashion. Hoped the other cowboys would think I was an outlaw.

"Once I was on night herd with one of the regular cowboys. Now, son, you've seen how they hold a herd at night." He gestured with a pipe stem. "One man goes around the herd in one direction, and the other man circles the other way. Slow and easy. And when you pass the other fellow, you have just time to say a few words. It keeps you awake. Well, on one round that night, the other cowboy asked me, 'Kid, what did you have to leave the settlements for?'

"We rode another circle, and when I met him again, I said, 'Don't like to say.' Another circle and he said, 'You never have said nothing since you been here—what've you done to have to leave?' We rode around again; then I swore him to secrecy. And still another circle. Then I confessed: 'I stole a steamboat.' We went around again. Then I said, 'And when I went back after the river, they came near catching me.' Well, he laughed so hard I thought he'd spook the herd, and after that I was in real good with the bunch.

25

"On quiet days, we'd lie around camp, and so I learned to play poker and monte. Then when we'd go to town, we'd have a real wild time, and come back broke. So I reckoned I was a real wild cowboy."

Why did that young man in 1888 feel that wildness meant being a cowboy? Why not a prospector or trapper or whaler or cavalryman or circus performer? Once I asked my grandfather, and he looked stumped. "Why, every kid wanted to be a cowboy – to prove that he had the stuff."

True enough. Old-time Oklahoma trail driver and rancher Jim Herron remarked that becoming a cowboy "was the dream of every Texas boy of my time from the hour he snagged his first hen or rooster with a twine loop. . . ."

South Dakotan Archer B. Gilfillan put it differently. Gilfillan was a sheepman, and noted the irony that a sheepherder's wages "run from ten to twenty dollars a month higher than the cowboy's in summer and are almost double the latter's in winter. But in spite of this, every kid in the range country looks forward to the day when he can . . . cultivate a bow-legged walk and hire out to a cattleman." The sheepman shows through as Gilfillan continues, ". . . cowboy stuff is merely a phase which boys pass through, like playing Indians or soldiers, only some of them never grow up. There will probably always be in the West a type of young fellow who cannot go out and drive in the milk cows without buckling on chaps and spurs."

I remember that type of swashbuckler from our family ranch. Overwhelmingly, our men were skilled and hardworking. And those with a touch of swagger had earned it honestly. But once in a while, poseurs ambled in. My father could usually spot them: Those with the fanciest rigs and the biggest rowels on their spurs generally spent but a brief time in our employ. Glamor tends to dissolve in sweat.

Our cowboys, of course, were Mexicans – *vaqueros* – so one must allow for the natural Latin dash. But since our first ranch, the Rancho Chuparosa, sat smack on the Rio Grande, we got a borderland blend of cowboy cultures. *Pochos,* the interior Mexicans called our kind; we scrambled English and Spanish, and mixed up our customs. I used to eat peanut butter on my tortillas, and I bathed – needfully – in tubfuls of the hard gypsum water from the Rio Grande itself.

In recollection, I can see what a strange life it was: some 2,000 beef cattle and 700 horses wearing the family Double X brand, plus about 10,000 slick-haired Mexican goats – tended by three goatherders, a *caporal* (foreman), a chuckwagon cook, and anywhere from six to a dozen vaqueros, depending on the season. All of us were plopped down on some 75,000 acres, which sounds larger than the rocky reality of cactus and mesquite brush. A neighboring ranch to the south, George Miers' Rancho San Miguel, covered more than a million acres and ran 40,000 cattle. I had then heard but remotely of the King Ranch. Today, its contiguous Texas acres near the Gulf of Mexico number one million – not counting other real estate scattered from Pennsylvania to Australia. And as a boy I had not heard at all of the Gang Ranch in Canada's British Columbia. There, along the muddy Fraser and the lucid Chilcotin Rivers, stretches what is surely the world's largest cattle ranch – a four-million-acre sweep of forest, mountain, and meadow some 75 miles across.

Still, the Chuparosa seemed big to me as a 5-year-old lured from the city. I learned to ride a burro, and finally graduated to some genuinely antique cow ponies, but it was years before I was permitted to ride with my father and the vaqueros. I didn't know enough to be grateful, not even in the dark of night when Mr. Williams —a foreman left over from the previous owners—would call out to my father from the screen porch: "Hobart! Time to get up. I see the morning star!"

Kindle a fire of dry sticks in the wood range, bake biscuits, fry ham and eggs, pour red-eye gravy over grits, fill cup after cup with steaming black coffee: then wait and wait for enough daylight to ride off on the day's rounds. Mr. Williams was a splendid man in many ways, sage in cowmanship, distinguished in the sweep of his big mustaches. His grooming was equivocal, though my grandfather told us his horse had once fallen into the river with him, thus positively documenting at least one bath. But an astronomer he was not, and each time we waited sleepily for daylight, his morning star seemed a far from heavenly body. When Mr. Williams finally tied up his bedroll and left for other parts, Father got more sleep. He simply employed a device—newfangled for the Chuparosa—called an alarm clock.

Father brought other innovations. Bright Coleman lanterns replaced some of the dim kerosene lamps. Registered Hereford bulls upgraded our *corriente,* scrub, stock. A battery-powered radio even brought us weather forecasts over station WOAI, San Antonio. We felt a need for weather news, for the border country, in those early years of the 1930's, was enduring one of its famous droughts.

"More cows have the creeps," Father would sigh as he dug the bootjack into his heel and heaved off his boots. The creeps meant a generally weakened condition caused by starvation. A cow grew skeletally thin, her pelvic bones lancing her hide; her back bowed and she took small, feeble steps. Soon we'd find that cow's carcass beneath a halo of turkey buzzards.

As the drought progressed into its second year, our water holes dried up. The Rio Grande grew thin and low, leaving a wide stinking stretch of slime along its banks. Wild game came from miles around to drink from the big river, losing even the fear of man. One afternoon I told my father how three deer had walked right past me. "They didn't run," I said. "I could have got one with my .22."

"We won't shoot deer like that," he said gently. "Wouldn't be fair. Besides," he added, trying to be gruff and practical, "they're all skinny now."

Preachers called prayer meetings to seek God's help. Stockmen studied the brassy sky with helpless, wishful bitterness, then with despair.

"The mares are grazing on the hill," our vaquero Prieto observed. "That always means rain." He also killed snakes and hung them on fences—another sure provider of rain. But my father quoted an old Texas saw: "All signs fail in dry weather."

So we hired more men and set crews to work chopping *sotol* roots with axes and burning thorns off prickly pear with blow torches. Cattle would follow the crews, eager to eat those sustaining morsels. I enjoyed watching the men do these jobs, but most of the time I simply played and learned boy's Spanish with my 6-year-old friend Celestino, the new foreman's son.

Elegantly dressed Mexican gentleman-horseman, or charro, *of about 1830 carries a sword at his saddle. He rides a light gray horse, a* tordillo.

Eventually, the drought ended—in gully-washing floods that stripped off top-soil and took out bridges. No matter. Cowboys could laugh once more.

Most of my ranch memories are happy ones: perched on the top board of the corral watching vaqueros break the green horses . . . asking questions while my friend Raúl plaited a horsehair rope or set a horseshoe . . . eating chunks of corn bread and barbecued goat meat cooked by old crippled Nacho at the chuckwagon . . . listening to the music on nights the men broke out guitars and sang. I recall the thrill I got when we moved our outfit from the Chuparosa to another ranch a few miles away, El Teniente. Life was easier, for now we had windmills and better water holes for the stock. We had running water in the house and, instead of the old zinc washtub, a white bathtub on claw-and-ball feet; I bathed less reluctantly. I even recall the prideful excitement of helping—or trying to—when calves were branded . . . and one great time riding on a spring roundup. Unfortunately, about the time I was old enough to be honestly useful, the family sold the ranch.

Yet through the years my interest in the cowboy life continued. I read history books by J. Frank Dobie, John A. Lomax, J. Evetts Haley, and Walter Prescott Webb. And whenever I ran across some old-time cowboy, I'd take notes and put his tales into a file drawer. But my interest lived strictly in spore form. As an East Coast father, I got my own youngsters some horses to ride—and, a bit guiltily, English saddles. But while a son or daughter hunted foxes, I read about the Old West and didn't ride a horse at all.

Then my work took me back to Texas. I saw a rodeo again, I talked to a few old-timers, and I met a whole generation of new-timers. And so I began to rediscover the cowboy. I realized that my own primitive boyhood experiences—in a kind of pre-electric, pre-windmill world—had given me a personal insight into a solid century of cowboy history. Now I found cattle ranching dramatically changed.

Cowboys earned more money, of course. "Yes, we pay a man $400 a month plus

*Early Texas rancher bears a rifle in a fringed scabbard slung from his saddle
horn. The* armas, *or leather apron, protects his legs from thorny mesquite.*

a house for his family and meat and maybe a milk cow and chickens," said rancher
Fred Boice, of Tucson, Arizona. "And still we have trouble getting good men. Maybe," he added, "we've lost all the fun out of ranching. With our nutritional advances,
gentle cattle, additional fencing—with all the changes, we don't even get to do any
roping. Not unless my son and I go out with ropes some Sunday afternoon for the
fun of it. In fact, we keep a few yearlings around just for that purpose."

Beneath the tall profile of Pikes Peak in Colorado, Tom Lasater stated flatly,
"We do no cowboying here. We don't even permit ropes on the saddles. If we find
an animal that needs attention, we bring it up to the house and use a squeeze chute."

In the Carmel Valley of California, Bob Wilson's 16-year-old son was gathering
Angus cows on a steep hillside—chugging around on his motorcycle.

Across the snowy expanses of Alberta, north of the frozen Red Deer River, I
spent one winter afternoon with Canadian Winston Bruce, rodeo manager of the
Calgary Stampede. A saddle-bronc champion, Winston that day was herding horses
with a snowmobile. "Saves people time around here," he said. So it does on the
Stampede organization's breeding ranch for bucking horses.

On a spring roundup for the Pitchfork Ranch, I soared into the Texas sky with
W. V. "Tuck" Blankenship in a helicopter. Below us, Billy George Drennan, Pitchfork wagon boss, and seven other cowboys brought in the cattle that we scared out of
the brush. Three of the men, I noticed, wore baseball caps instead of big-brimmed hats.

"Easier for driving in a pickup," Billy George explained later. "Now let's see.
We've got 130 head here. We could have worked that pasture three days and not
had that many. Helicopters save us lots of miles on the ground."

Even rustling has changed. "Used to be, it took a cowboy to steal a cow,"
said Amarillo brand inspector W. I. "Red" Bennett. "Now cattle are so gentle anybody can do it. Just throw some feed into a truck, and the old cow goes right in."

But another change seemed even more fundamental. Said cattleman Van Irvine in Buffalo, Wyoming: "I just can't get men to work as cowboys now. Most of the seasonal help I get is girls. That's right. In summer, most of my cowboys are girls."

Van's employees aren't entirely typical, but it's true that able cowboys are hard for ranchers to find — in spite of a shrinking need.

"Back in the 1930's," said manager Swede Nelson of Wyoming's Snake River Ranch, "our place had seven or eight cowboys. Now we only need four or five."

On many a well-run ranch these days, you can see the cowboys leave for a roundup in a truck. Their horses, already saddled, follow in a gooseneck trailer. On arrival at the pasture they will work, the men unload the horses and mount up. "We can save a long day's ride that way," Pitchfork manager Jim Humphreys said. "And we can work another pasture next day."

Thus ranches need fewer cowboys and fewer horses. Historians Joe B. Frantz and Julian Choate have estimated that in the heyday of trail-driving some 40,000 men worked as cowboys in U. S. territories. Today, there are probably no more than half that number.

I've met a few thousand of them over the years. They have come in all colors, sizes, and scales of quality. Yet, like cowpuncher E. C. "Teddy Blue" Abbott, I too "would know an old cowboy in hell with his hide burnt off. It's the way they stand and walk and talk." In Paducah, Texas, Carl Darr builds saddles with narrow, 12-inch cantles because, as he puts it, "The men here in the big-ranch country are slimmer in the hips." In Fort Pierre, South Dakota, Tom Hughes points out a cowhand "with a face like whang leather" — the wrinkling effects of wind and sun. But the sunburn is localized. On rare occasions when a cowboy takes off his hat, his forehead seems nudely white. "Like Indian sign language," adds my friend Dorothy Mondell Frame. "I learned it as a girl in Wyoming. The sign for white man was to pass fingers across the forehead."

But whatever their appearance, the cowboys I've known have overwhelmingly, as my grandfather perceived, been men who had the stuff.

Casey Tibbs makes a similar point. We'd been talking about his rodeo tour of Japan, and the Japanese enthusiasm for cowboys. How, I wondered, did he explain the worldwide appeal of the cowboy as folk hero? "Self-reliance may have something to do with it. . . ." Casey has lost that kindergarten look he wore on a *Life* magazine cover in 1951. Now, in his 40's, this legendary rodeo champion has a face as round as a Western toby jug. "I've thought about it," he said. "You could take me in a plane and drop me just about anywhere. And I know that — *somehow* — I'd make out. . . . Maybe the American cowboy represents the last of the free men."

Perhaps, then, freedom is the cowboy's appeal. "But, Dad," my 19-year-old son Kelly admonishes me, "cowboys just aren't romantic." He spent last summer working in Wyoming as a horse wrangler, the lowest rung on the social ladder of any cattle ranch. He was the only college student working there, and his colleagues were generally the too-young or the too-old — "and the too-dirty," Kelly adds. "You just can't stay clean. Nope, not romantic at all."

But then Kelly talks about one old sidekick named Jess, half Apache and half

Irish, who came from Arizona and had punched cows all over the West "until he entered a saddle-bronc event in some rodeo and caught his spur in the cinch. Horse went over on his leg and crushed it. So he walks stiff-legged now. He goes to work wearing fancy spurs that he won in a dice game and some $100 Paul Bond boots. But he uses the same razor blade for months — sharpens it on the inside of a glass. Imagine: half Apache and half Irish. Wonder which is wilder."

Or which is less romantic? Yet I remember Dan Fowler, a young Nevada cowboy — or buckaroo, as Nevadans say. Dan was packing up his gear to move from one ranch line camp to another, muttering complaints with every armload. "I've got enough junk here for *five women*," he said. But in addition to his rig and well-filled bedroll, he reserved room for one special treasure: a boxed edition of paintings by cowboy-artist Charles M. Russell. "Yeah, I have three of Russell's books — but just one with me here."

Dan learned the cowboy arts while still a toddler perched on the horn of his mother's saddle, so perhaps he should take for granted the whole buckaroo life. Yet he reads cowboy-author Will James and collects Charlie Russells.

"It's like feedback on the PA system," my father used to say. Horse operas and dime novels come out of the ranch country and then make a round trip, recruiting more cowboys.

As early as 1886 — while the great trail drives were still in progress — this nostalgic passage appeared in Harper's *New Monthly Magazine:*

"The Texas cowboys were frontiersmen, accustomed from their earliest childhood to forays of Indians of the most ferocious nature. The sections in the state where they lived were also exposed to incursions of bandits from Mexico.... By virtue of their courage and recklessness of danger, their excellent horsemanship, and skill in the use of firearms, they have been an efficient instrumentality in protecting the frontier settlements...."

Young men of the late 19th century read such prose and wanted to head out West. The ranch hand himself read it and he thought of himself as "a real wild cowboy," in my grandfather's phrase.

Author Charlie Siringo used to quote a letter he received from Will Rogers: "Somebody gave me the proof sheet of your new book [*Riata and Spurs*].... and wanted to know what I think of it.... I think the same of it as I do the first cowboy book I ever read, *Fifteen Years on the Hurricane Deck of a Spanish Pony* [also by Siringo]. Why, that was the Cowboy's Bible when I was growing up. I camped with a herd one night at the old LX Ranch, just north of Amarillo in '98, and they showed me an old forked tree where some old bronc had bucked you into. Why, that to us was like looking at the Shrine of Shakespeare to some of these 'deep foreheads.'...."

So the cowboy legend tugs at its own bootstraps. Does that mean Will Rogers and Charlie Siringo represent counterfeit cowboys? And what do we mean by the term cowboy, anyhow?

Well, we don't mean the Revolutionary War foragers who "often made excursions to get fresh beef, and hence were called 'Cow-boys.'" So wrote one "individual witness of those desperate times." The expression *cow-boy* may be 18th century, but the cowboy way of life is not.

By cowboy I don't mean a cattle baron or a Western gunslinger. A cowboy is simply a man who plies the crafts of the cattle ranch; he can be owner or hired hand — though he doesn't need to remain either all his life.

And here we collide with something that Drs. Frantz and Choate call the "distinctly Texas cast" that surrounded the early cowboy. Their book, *The American Cowboy: The Myth and the Reality,* warily nods to those folk grown weary "of the professionally garrulous Texan," but they make this point: "True, cowboys showed up all over the plains areas, but it was the Texas cowboy who taught his northern cousin the techniques of handling cattle in the vastnesses of open range.... The Montana cowboy was a legitimate copy of the Texas cowboy, but he was just that, a copy of the original." And they cite the early chroniclers to affirm "that the cattlemen's frontier was a Texas story from beginning to end."

For example, we have mentioned Charlie Siringo. He was born in south Texas on "a bright morning on the 7th day of February 1856," as he put it. His Italian father died when Charlie was only a year old. But his Irish mother got him started in school at age 4, in "a little old frame building" where he "had to hoof it ... through the grassburrs, barefooted.... Crowds of Cow Boys used to come over ... to rope wild steers in my presence — hence me trying to imitate them."

Soon he was butchering an occasional maverick; Charlie defines the term:

"In early days, a man by the name of Mavrick [Samuel A. Maverick] ... started a cow ranch. He being a chicken-hearted old rooster, wouldn't brand nor ear-mark any of his cattle. All his neighbors branded theirs, therefore Mr. Mavrick claimed everything that wore long ears.

"When the war broke out [the Civil War] Mr. Mavrick had to bid adieu to wife and babies and go far away to fight for his country's good.

"When the cruel war was ended, he went home and found his cattle roaming over a thousand hills....

"But when his neighbors ... came home and went to branding their five years increase, Mr. Mavrick did not feel so rich. He made a terrible fuss about it, but it did no good, as in a very few years his cattle wore some enterprising man's brand and he was left out in the cold."

Hence the term maverick for any unbranded range animal.

At age 15, Charlie hired out to Texas cattleman Abel Head "Shanghai" Pierce and his Rancho Grande — literally a big ranch since "the next year ... we branded twenty-five thousand calves." Young Charlie "spent two or three months' wages for an outfit, spurs, etc., trying to make myself look like a thoroughbred Cow Boy from Bitter Creek."

The cattle business was undergoing some marked changes in those years. Railroads were pushing westward, and Texas cattlemen had begun to drive their animals north to the railroad towns of Kansas. Lanky Longhorns had once been butchered just for their hide and tallow ("the meat he threw to the hogs," Charlie says of one rancher). Now, a $2 Longhorn could bring $10 on a new nationwide cattle market.

In 1874, when Charlie was 18, he made his first trail drive across the Red River and Indian Territory on the Chisholm Trail.

"My wages were thirty-five dollars per month and all expenses," he wrote, "including railroad fare back home." His herd included 1,100 head "of wild and woolly steers . . . mostly of Kansas 'short horns.'. . . We were almost worn out standing night guard half of every night. . . . [one] night it began to storm terribly. . . . The steers showed a disposition to stampede but we handled them easy and sang melodious songs which kept them quieted. But about one o'clock they stampeded in grand shape. . . . the herd split up into a dozen different bunches — each bunch going in a different direction. I found myself all alone with about three hundred of the frightened steers. . . . I finally about three o'clock got them stopped and after singing a few 'lullaby' songs they all lay down and went to snoring."

That wasn't Charlie's only problem; he quarreled with the trail boss, "a regular old sore-head" who wanted Siringo and a sidekick to ride wild horses along the way. "We finally bolted and told him that we wouldn't ride another wild horse . . . unless he gave us extra pay." So "in Fayette county I got the bounce. . . . He hired other men in our places. He arrived in Wichita, Kansas, with eight hundred steers, out of the eleven hundred we started with." Charlie fared little better, for he met "two young Misses," and "began to get light in the pocket. . . . After buying and rigging up a saddle I left town flat broke. I spent my last dime for a glass of lemonade. . . ."

During some 15 years of cowboying, Siringo spent his wages in other ways. Feeling like "an old stove-up cowpuncher" (though still shy of 30), he bought a Kansas hardware store and wrote his memoirs of life in the saddle, a book that became a national best seller and the volume Will Rogers considered the Cowboy's Bible. He then joined the Pinkerton's National Detective Agency and spent more than 20 years chasing outlaws. But his cowboy career remains the most memorable for two reasons: He was the first cowboy to write his own story; and his work spanned much of the Golden Age of the cowboy — roughly from the end of the Civil War in 1865 to 1890. This was the time when Texas began to export both its beef and its cowboy lore to the rest of the country.

"But long before 1865, you Texans learned how to tend cattle from us," says my friend Luís Hernández, a prominent *ganadero* — or beef raiser — of central Mexico. "Even your Longhorns originated with the Spanish corriente cattle."

In the clear sunshine of Querétaro, Luís presides over eleven family and corporate farms, an enterprise that supports more than 5,000 employees and residents in the hacienda villages. One of those employees is Jesús Esquivel, a skilled vaquero.

"I'm 55 years old," asserts Jesús.

"Don't let his pious name fool you," adds Luís. "Jesús lies. He's really 65. And he has three wives."

"But in different houses," Jesús cackles. "Though all on this hacienda."

And what is his work here?

"I take care of the fighting bulls — and also Don Luís," jokes Jesús.

"He does nothing but drink *pulque,*" says Luís. "You know it? A brew made from cactus juice, very strong."

"No, Don Luís," says Jesús. "I fight with the man who sells pulque." But soon Luís leaves me alone to chat with Jesús, and the amiable vaquero produces an earthen jar, or *olla,* full of cool pulque. In the feathery shade of a *pirul* tree, we sip and talk.

"Yes, Don Luís gives me one saddle each year and my sombrero and ropes, plus 30 pesos a day"—about $2.40—"and food and a place to live.... Well, yes! For me, *three* places to live." He laughs, exposing a nearly complete set of his own teeth. "Our families eat well—corn, beans, meat, coffee, milk...whatever the hacienda produces. Other things we buy in town."

His day begins about 5 a.m. when Jesús rises, takes a cup of coffee, "and sometimes a little glass of pulque," and mounts his horse to make his rounds. Later, he eats a breakfast of eggs and chili. Lunch might be beans and meat wrapped in tortillas, and supper is more of the same.

In spite of siestas and small talk, this vaquero works hard. And Jesús Esquivel enjoys some regional fame in Querétaro for his prowess with the rope, his easy command of horses, and his understanding of cattle. Does he like the life?

"Here the life is happy, or it's sad," he muses. "But the life is never alone. You have people with you."

For the convivial Mexican vaquero, there can be no better way to live. And perhaps that's the biggest contrast with the life of the Anglo-cowboy farther north.

Consider John Ballard, the best roper on the Pitchfork Ranch in the Texas Panhandle. John is 70, slim, and quiet. "Got a match, John?" somebody asks.

"Sure," he drawls. "I may go out without my britches, but I've always got my matches." Over a full meal John will impart an encyclopedia of range wisdom. How does he keep Brahmans—BRAY-mas, as cattlemen call them—from running away into the brush? "You can tie those old Brayma horns—tighten them up so you can hear those horns pop. The horns will be so tender you can't *run* 'em into brush."

"A MONTANA TYPE"

"THE SCOUT"

Rugged and self-reliant, men of the Old West proved themselves equal to the challenges of frontier life. From left: An Arizona cow-poke holds a loop at the ready; a bandanna masks a stage robber armed with shotgun and pistol; an old-style Texas cowman wears fringed buckskin; goat-hair "angoras" help keep a Montanan warm in winter; an Army scout cradles his repeating rifle.

John sings the praises of his fellow cowboys: "Yeah, that old boy is rough all right. He can beat you to death playing with you, but he'll take his shirt off and give it to you if he thinks you need it." Still, if you want to know something about John himself, he goes shy and mute, so you need to visit his wife Mabel. They live at Croton Camp, a remote frame house with a sulphuric water supply half a day's horseback ride from the Pitchfork headquarters.

"It had belonged to the Matador Ranch when we first moved in," Mabel recalls. "That was 24 years ago. Weeds—you couldn't see the yard fence. No electricity or running water. We used a wood range, but a good one. I haven't made a decent biscuit since we got this new stove. I knew just how many sticks of wood I needed to bake an angel food cake. When we got the well and cistern and the bathroom and electricity, I told John I thought I was getting more than I deserved.

"We still have power failures sometimes—you know, a bobcat may tangle with an insulator. But now I can't hardly see by a coal-oil lamp anymore.

"I used to trap bobcats down on the river here. And I always had to take the .22 and kill them myself. John wouldn't. He won't kill any living thing."

What about the isolation of their life at Croton Camp? "One time, years ago when they were branding, there was two weeks—Sundays and all—that I didn't see another face but John's. And I only saw his face after dark and before daylight, he worked so long. And during that time I was younger and just didn't care.

"Later, for a while, I resented it—being away from all my people—when John is past retirement age. But John's miserable when he's not doing something.

"You know he came back home the other evening after they'd been branding. He'd just roped and roped that day. And telling me about it when he come home, John just started to grin, and then he turned so *red.* This boy had told John, 'I always thought my daddy was the best roper, but,' he says, 'you've taken it away from him.'

"John wanted to tell me that so bad. Not to brag—but because he wants to be doing his part.

"Yes, both of us love the outdoors; the river here is so pretty. I walk a lot. And for my tranquilizers, I work outside. There's been more happiness here than the other way. . . ."

More than geography separates John Ballard — blushing when he repeats a compliment to his wife — and the outgoing, picaresque Jesús Esquivel. Yet I can't imagine either of these skilled old ropers being happy in another kind of job.

"I've tried driving a truck, even tending bar, but that almost drove me up the wall," said Ron Willis, of the Snake River Ranch. "You cuss the hot, and you cuss the cold. But something always keeps pulling you back."

Ron — an energetic mixture of Irish, English, and Sioux — comes from the western slopes of Colorado. "I've always liked the mountains because — well, the son-of-a-guns are *home.* You know our tall grass? Indian word for it is *piceance.* It's piceance country. And that grass is really tall; you can ride through it and shine your boots."

As we talked, Ron rested in a meadow beneath the snows of the Tetons. He walked over to the shade of an aspen, deep grass muting the jangle of his spurs. Then he poured some coffee from a Thermos, sprawled full length, and fanned himself with a sweat-soiled hat. "Yes. That $20 hat needs a $10 cleaning." The band, I noticed, carried a supply of hypodermic needles pinned and ready for vaccine. "That coffee's strong," he said approvingly. "You could cut a plug off of that coffee. . . . When I was 25, I could fall out of bed, eat two chickens and half a loaf of bread — no problems. Can't now. I'm 31. Yes, sir, people get wound up with the world. But you know, I can still lay down right here and sleep like a baby."

Ron's comments remind me of another man who recalled his first days on the prairie and "the spell from which . . . I may never emerge." This was L. A. Huffman, Iowa-born farmboy and sometime cattle rancher, who moved to Fort Keogh in Montana Territory in the winter of 1878 as post photographer. "I made photographs," Huffman said in summary of his life's work. "With crude homemade cameras, from saddle and in log shack, I saved something."

But was Huffman himself a cowboy? Well, he earned his first wages at 13 by riding herd on some Iowa cattle, and he first met the prairie when his boss sent him on a 30-mile errand mounted on a spirited little mare. "Never can I forget the feelings . . . that day . . . ," he wrote, "once the mare . . . had carried me far out upon that billowing plain. . . ." He spent his first night in the wide-open spaces; he leaned for a time on the mare's neck and wondered what she saw "with her long, far away listing gaze into the depths of that gathering night." Next morning, he heard her whinny. "A horseman was approaching. . . . Now enter the hero of my boyish dreams, the plainsman, the first of his kind my eyes had ever beheld. . . . Mustang Ben, with the great tawny beard . . . was dismounting before me and offering 'Good Morning' and the grasp of his hard, hairy hand. Tales of his adventures and prowess in bringing bands of wild horses for barter out of the border of the buffalo and Indian land had fired my imagination long before.

"Everything dates from that chance meeting. Ben and his wild riders and herd of mustangs were going my way to sell ponies. . . ." So Huffman went west and stayed

52 years. He branded his stock with H-Lazy-L, and shared his outdoor life with cowboys named Itchy Jake, Six Shooter Bob, and Never Slip. He got to know Indians like Rain-in-the-Face and Fire Wolf. But most of all, he took pictures.

"I just returned ... from a 12 days ride with the Powder River Roundup," he once wrote his father. "I shall soon show you what can be done from the saddle without ground glass or tripod ... many of the best [were] exposed while my horse was in motion...." Huffman stayed in motion himself. And thus he made some of the greatest, most honest pictures of the beef traffic. But would cowmen consider Huffman a cowboy? I asked a 71-year-old cowhand in the Big Horn Mountains.

"Just look at his pictures," he replied. "Only a cowboy could have done them."

Then what about an asthmatic young Harvard man who left his New York home in 1883 to find solace and good health on a North Dakota cattle ranch? Years later, he recalled the "kind of idyl" he knew in the short-grass country.

"It was still the Wild West in those days, the Far West ... a land of vast silent spaces, of lonely rivers, and of plains where the wild game stared at the passing horseman. It was a land of scattered ranches, of herds of long-horned cattle, and of reckless riders who unmoved looked in the eyes of life or death. In that land we led a free and hardy life, with horse and with rifle. We worked under the scorching midsummer sun, when the wide plains shimmered and wavered in the heat; and we knew the freezing misery of riding night guard round the cattle in the late fall round-up.... We knew toil and hardship and hunger and thirst; and we saw men die violent deaths as they worked among the horses and cattle, or fought in evil feuds with one another; but we felt the beat of hardy life in our veins, and ours was the glory of work and the joy of living."

So wrote Theodore Roosevelt in his autobiography. Perhaps he said it better — and more spontaneously — in a speech he made in Sioux Falls, South Dakota, in 1910:

"My friends ... it was here that I lived a number of years in a ranch house in the cattle country, and I regard my experience during those years, when I lived and worked with my own fellow ranchmen on what was then the frontier, as the most important educational asset of all my life. It is a mighty good thing to know men, not from looking at them, but from having been one of them."

Well, maybe. But young Teddy Roosevelt didn't become an authentic cowboy overnight. On one early roundup, this bespectacled Easterner actually shouted, "Hasten forward quickly there!" The cowboys broke up laughing.

Gradually, though, Roosevelt won their respect. He started a ranch of his own near Medora, North Dakota. He survived a fall from a 40-foot cliff, a broken shoulder, and the threat of a duel — his rival begged off.

Once Roosevelt even made up a posse of two friends, went off through the wildest parts of the Badlands, and captured three outlaws. During the last 36 hours of that ordeal, Roosevelt kept a rifle trained on his prisoners as they all walked, with little rest and no sleep, for 40 miles.

Of his Dakota hardships, the ever-buoyant Roosevelt exclaimed, "By Godfrey but this is fun!" He found "the moral tone of a cow camp ... rather high." And he praised the "hardy and self-reliant" cowboys. The admiration came to be requited.

"A plumb good sort," his hunting guide called Roosevelt. On that judgment, surely, we can count T. R. a cowboy.

When in 1902 writer Owen Wister completed *The Virginian,* the first best-selling cowboy novel, he dedicated it to his friend Theodore Roosevelt. Like the narrator of his book and T. R. himself, Wister was an Easterner who had gone West and discovered a new way of life.

Wister's first reaction to cowboys was guarded: "I'm told they're without any moral sense whatever." But as he met more cowboys his knowledge and regard grew — and turned into unaffected hero worship.

"All America is divided into two classes — the quality and the equality. . . . Both will be with us until our women bear nothing but kings," wrote Wister in *The Virginian.* Cowboys — at least a portion of them, he insisted — represented the quality class. Certainly his Virginia-born hero did. This is the way readers met him, in wordless action:

"I saw near the track an enclosure, and round it some laughing men, and inside it some whirling dust, and amid the dust some horses, plunging, huddling, and dodging. They were cow ponies in a corral, and one of them would not be caught, no matter who threw the rope. . . . Through the window-glass of our Pullman the thud of their mischievous hoofs reached us, and the strong, humorous curses of the cowboys. Then for the first time I noticed a man who sat on the high gate of the corral, looking on. For he now climbed down with the undulations of a tiger, smooth and easy, as if his muscles flowed beneath his skin. . . . I did not see his arm lift or move. He appeared to hold the rope down low, by his leg. But like a sudden snake I saw the noose go out its length and fall true; and the thing was done. As the captured pony walked in with a sweet, church-door expression, our train moved slowly on to the station, and a passenger remarked, 'That man knows his business.' "

Does Wister over-romanticize this cowboy? No more, I think, than cowboys romanticize themselves. As Exhibit A, I submit my Uncle Bert's ivory-handled pistol — how he loved to show it off to visiting Easterners!

Faithful chronicler that he was, Wister caught the flavor of cowboy pranks and high jinks. His paragon mischievously switches all the babies around at a country dance. And that prank seems quite in character for other cowboys. Charlie Russell and his friend in the Montana Judith Basin, for example, once got hold of some Limburger cheese.

"We rubbed it on doorknobs, bar-rails, beer glasses and hatbands," Russell later reported. "Soon we had about everything pretty well stunk up with it. None of us was civilized 'nough to have a taste for the stuff. We'd about run out of places to daub when we saw an old-timer named Bill, who'd taken on too much joy juice and was sleepin' it off in the corner of the saloon by the stove.

"Well, the old nester's heavy, droopin' moustache gave one of the boys a right bright idea. A council was held, and we decided Bill shouldn't be deprived of his share of the cheese, so we rubbed it into his moustache right under his nose.

Firm grasp on their horses' tails eases the climb for a party of hunters in New Mexico. The practice caused little discomfort to the mounts —Mexican vaqueros at first tied their lariats to their horses' tails. They soon shifted the rope to the pommel for greater safety in roping the wild Longhorn.

"He slept peaceful-like till the next mornin'. I was out back of the saloon when I heard the ... groanin'. There was Bill settin' on a box, lookin' mighty sad. He'd raise his cupped hands to his mouth, breathe heavy-like, and drop his hands and then start groanin'.

" 'Bill,' I says, 'how you feelin' this mornin'?'

" 'Keep away from me, I'm dyin',' he says waving me back.

" 'What's the matter?' I asks. 'You sick, Bill?'

" 'No, I've felt as bad as this a thousand times,' says Bill, 'but this is awful. I'm goin' to die sure 'cause no man can live long with this awful breath. I'm plumb spoiled inside. I'm dyin' sure.'

"And you know I believe he'd died, too, if I hadn't told him. He got well in a hurry and got good and ringey when he found out what was ailin' him."

Typical cowboy high jinks. For all the rawhide humor, however, the cowboy had the serious moods of a natural loner with few but important friends.

"Tommie Clayton, one of my best friends, and I rode a lot together," Matthew Hooks recalled. Hooks was a black man with the nickname of Bones. But his friendship for white Tommie Clayton crossed all barriers. "Tommie's people lived at Pecos, but Tommie was one of these boys who liked the open country and horses and cattle. Tommie's horse fell and hurt him pretty bad, and he had to be taken to town. Two or three days from then one of the boys was going to town so I went out and picked a bouquet of white flowers that Tommie liked so well and asked the boy to take them to my friend, thinking this would cheer him up and remind him of the happy days we rode together. The cowboy said, 'Suppose he is dead?' I just said, 'Put them on his grave if he is.' When the flowers got there, Tommie was dead and the flowers were put on his grave. There was almost another funeral the next time I went to town and saw Tommie's people."

Three times in the 1930's Bones Hooks was interviewed by university history students. Their scholarly transcripts are on file with the extraordinary western collection of the Panhandle-Plains Historical Society in Canyon, Texas.

"I never worked as a cow hand on a ranch," said Bones, explaining the pecking order of his outfits. "I was just supposed to break horses."

Cowhand or not, nobody on the plains of Texas ever doubted that Bones was a cowboy and a fine one. Born in Robertson County, Texas, to former slaves in 1867, he started work as a wagon driver at the age of "about seven or eight...."

"I was just a little kid when I came to this country.... I was riding a mule one day when Mr. Norris came along in his wagon. He asked me if I were a cowboy and I said, 'Yes.' He said that cowboys didn't ride mules, and if I would come with him, he would trade me five ponies for my mule. ... So I said, 'Right here's where you get traded off, old mule.' So I went with him and began riding horses. I stayed there about two or three years.... I liked the Pecos country.... The cowboys would put me on the horses and they would throw me off before I hardly got in the saddle, but the boys kept putting me on them and the horses kept throwing me off, until finally they could find none that I could not ride."

How much did he earn after he learned to break horses? "I got about $3.00 a head or $25.00 a month with board." And what did he do for recreation? "I was working all of the time.... There was no Sunday. Lots of times a man would not know what day of the week it was. You lose time ... out on the range with just a bunch of men for ninety days. It would be just daylight and night."

What about racial prejudice in the late 19th century? Here Bones told of an experience he had in east Texas at Wamba. "I opened a store there and run it about 18 months. One day I come in and found a sign on my door which read, 'We give you 36 hours to get out,' signed by 'White Caps of Sand Gall Gizzard.' I give 'em 33 hours of that back." But out in the ranch country, attitudes differed: "In this country have lived the very strongest of characters.... the best people. I worked on the railroad for 20 years, and having always looked for the brand on cattle and horses, I always looked for some kind of a mark on men. I never found anything to compare with the people on the Plains. I could always tell them, by their walk or the way they looked . . . .

"When a man came to this country . . . he would ride all day without any water sometimes, and if he did not use a little horse sense, he could not stand it for long. He soon learned to tell where there was water and where there was no water. He would watch the birds and see which way they were flying in the early morning. He learned that the birds flew to water in the morning and from it in the late evening. If he found himself in a place where there was no birds, no life of any sort, and no trails, he knew there was no water around there. He could find his directions from the way the wind was blowing, for it nearly always blew from the Southwest. If a man was going to stay here, he had to look for these things in order to live. . . . First there was the buffalo trail, which was before my time, then the cattle and wagons went over the trail, and now you have the paved highway."

Thus black cowboy Bones Hooks summed up the story of progress in the cattle country, as of 1933. But he added one rueful memory: "We got supplies for the ranches with freight wagons. . . . We saw something then you all are not going to see. I have seen a wagon loaded with groceries, sitting in a wagon yard without having anybody bother it while the owner was gone. If you don't tie the auto down now, when you come back it is gone."

Along with open honesty the cowboy sometimes — and a bit self-consciously — shows a religious side of his nature. In the old days, camp meetings and revivals became exciting social events. "We stopped over Sunday in the little Christian Colony and went to church," notes Charlie Siringo. "The Rev. Cahart preached about the wild and woolly Cow Boy of the west; how the eastern people had him pictured off as a kind of animal with horns, etc. While to him, looking down from his dry goods box pulpit into the manly faces of nearly a hundred of them, they looked just like human beings, minus the standing collar, etc."

Sometimes, though, piety rests uncomfortably upon the cowboy. Once at a Nevada line camp I heard a buckaroo suddenly emit a whole barrage of oaths. "What's the matter?" I asked.

He swore again. "I just remembered it's Sunday. And I've missed church."

A Texan seemed more casual. "Yeah, I got baptized," he told me. "But I guess the water wasn't hot enough."

This duality of good and bad has forever been part of the cowboy's reputation. "They strike terror to the heart of the population," wrote a Spanish inspector in early colonial Mexico, ". . . and most of them are equipped with breastplates, harquebuses, scythes . . . and other weapons."

Yet the pious Father Alonso Ponce explained the daring exploits of a cowboy from Jalisco "in order to glorify and praise God, who bestows on His creatures such courage, strength, and skill."

My grandfather hit the keynote: "Most anything you want to say about cowboys is true. But the important thing is, they take care of cows."

2

No Trail Too Rough or Long

THROUGHOUT MY BOYHOOD on the ranch, I nursed a single big regret: that I missed one 30-mile trail drive from the ranch to Ciudad Acuña. We had sold a herd of half-breed Brahmans for export to the United States. Instead of riding with the vaqueros, I had to settle for the tales they told about that journey.

"*¡Qué cosa! ¡Qué barbaridad!* What a barbarity!" Prieto exclaimed when he reported to my father. "The wild Brahman cow gored my horse yesterday—there, you see? And tried to kill me. Oh, they would not be herded." He swore richly for a while. "It has taken us a week to come these few kilometers. And who knows what will happen when we enter the city?"

Acuña had perhaps 5,000 people, but our wild-eyed Brahmans had never before seen even a village. I asked Father to let me watch the herd come into town.

"If you can talk your grandfather into taking you (*Continued on page 71*)

Sweat-stained and bone-tired after a day of chasing down strays, 33-year-old Benny Butler of the Pitchfork Ranch reins in his horse for a brief rest late on a sunny spring afternoon on the high plains of the Texas big-ranch country.

"THE OLD TIME COW PUNCHER": COWBOY WATCHES CATTLE FROM THE SHADE OF HIS HORSE.

Cresting a hill, cattle from the Snake River Ranch in Wyoming start a 60-mile drive

to summer pasture. Ranch manager Swede Nelson rides lead, trailed by his dog Mel.

Snow-splotched mountains of Wyoming's Teton Range loom
in late-afternoon haze as Snake River cattle plod through
sagebrush, grazing as they move. Blocking the road (top), the
herd trails across U. S. Highway 89 during the seven-day drive.
When the stock—380 cows and 360 calves—bedded down
nearby, a passing motorist struck and killed a calf. Above,
Swede Nelson—behind horse—and ranch hand Ron Willis
load a fresh mount, saddled and ready for work. Pickup trucks
provide quick transport for men, horses, and sick or lame cows.

Riding Ginger, a top cutting horse, Snake River cowboy Don Park gets set to drop a loop over a calf afflicted with the scours—dysentery. After "doctoring," the calf will rejoin its mother. Occasionally, however, a cow will abandon her offspring. By lantern light, Swede Nelson holds a deserted calf while Ron Willis feeds it condensed milk and water from a paper cup. "Luckily, we got this little fellow together with a cow whose calf had died," Swede recalls. "But we had to help out. Since cows identify their calves by smell, we sprayed the calf with deodorant and gave the cow a noseful. It worked because she came to accept the calf by that scent." At midnight, Ron Willis relaxes with a cup of coffee, listening for unusual sounds among the cattle. When the herd finally settles down, Ron can grab a short rest—the drive will resume long before sunup.

Smoke from seared hide veils Don Park as he burns the Lazy R-R brand of the Snake River Ranch across the ribs of a month-old calf. Tilted to its side and roped by its hind legs, a bawling calf (below) lies stretched on a branding table; a full crew of six men can brand 55 calves an hour. Ranch hands mark, vaccinate, castrate, and dehorn calves at one to two months of age. After a long morning's work, hungry men break for a noon meal of beef, biscuits, gravy, potatoes, and greens at ranch headquarters.

Longhorns bound for Kansas ford the Red River at Doan's Store on the Western Trail.

"DOAN'S CROSSING," BY CHARLIE DYE, 1970, PRIVATE COLLECTION

Between 1878 and 1885, millions of animals crossed here from Texas to Indian Territory.

Buyers for feedlots and packing plants crowd the auction barn at the Fort Worth Stockyards, bidding on feeder calves as they trot around the ring. On a busy day, 8,000 animals may change hands. As bidders compete, waiting cattle-truck drivers (right) relax in the top rows. A stock worker on a trail bike (opposite) moves cattle toward the auction ring—a method first used at these Texas yards.

Sprawling across 360 acres near Canyon, Texas, the Randall County Feedlot pens 65,000

cattle—5,000 fewer than its capacity—to fatten before being shipped to slaughterhouses.

First breed of cattle to range North America, the tough and self-sufficient Longhorn arrived with early Spanish explorers, multiplied, and eventually formed the great wild herds of Texas. Later settlers imported more placid cattle from the British Isles, including the Shorthorn (above), the white-faced Hereford, and the black Aberdeen Angus—all excellent beef animals. The cream-colored French Charolais, a thick, muscular animal used in crossbreeding, first came to the United States in 1935.

PAINTING BY JAY MATTERNES

Crossing European and Asian stock, American ranchers have developed breeds of cattle stressing weight, hardiness, disposition, and early maturity. These distinctive United States breeds include the humped Brahman (left) descended from zebu cattle of India; the Santa Gertrudis (above) of the Texas King Ranch, a blend of Brahman and Shorthorn; the black Brangus of Brahman and Angus lineage; the Beefmaster of the Lasater Ranch in Colorado, a mixture of Hereford, Shorthorn, and Brahman.

PAINTING BY JAY MATTERNES

Wild and unbroken progeny of rodeo broncs and soured saddle mounts, a horse herd thunders down an embankment in South Dakota, spooked by riders brandishing coiled ropes. Each spring cowboys round up about 150 of the outlaw animals from a herd of several hundred, drive them 65 miles to Fort Pierre, and auction them as bucking stock for rodeos. Casey Tibbs (left), owner of the horses and seven times world saddle-bronc champion, savors snuff in his upper lip as he watches cowboys at work on the drive.

Jarring cartwheel ends a brief and turbulent bareback ride at the Miles City, Montana, Bucking Horse Sale, an exhibit and auction for rodeo stock contractors. In billowing dust, cowboys saddle an obstinate bronc; one man must mount it and try to cross a finish line. A young contestant gets encouragement in a quiet moment before his ride. Most of the competitors work on nearby ranches.

PAINTING BY O. E. BERNINGHAUS, C. 1910, KENNEDY GALLERIES, INC., NEW YORK

"The Forgotten": Neglected cow ponies stand with lowered heads in a cover of snow

outside a Colorado saloon. Dependent on their mounts, cowboys usually treated them well.

"Separating colts from their mothers to brand and halter-break them is some of the hardest work we do," says Jim Humphreys of the Pitchfork Ranch in Texas. Above, a Quarter Horse mare shields her two-month-old colt as ranch hands try to part them. After branding it on the cheek, a cowboy paints on healing linseed oil and lime. A colt already halter-broken stands quietly; within two years he will feel the weight of a saddle for the first time.

Rearing bareback bronc tries to pitch off a rodeo rider in a sport that evolved from "home entertainment" on early-day ranches.

"PAYWINDOW," BY ROBERT SCRIVER, 1971, COLLECTION OF NATIONAL COWBOY HALL OF FAME, OKLAHOMA CITY

in the car, O.K.," said Father. "But stay in the car." Grandfather readily agreed. "I'll keep you company," he said. "Nobody with any sense would meet those snaky cows on foot."

We parked near the Acuña main street where we had a view of Las Vacas Creek. "It ought to be something, watching them cross," Grandfather said.

But they didn't cross as a herd. Before the Brahmans got into town something scared them, perhaps the sight of the town itself. They splintered into half a dozen crazy segments and pounded in like racehorses.

"Hot dog!" cried my grandfather. "We don't have one stampede. We've got six!" One bunch splashed across the shallow creek, whipping the water to spray. Others dashed down the causeway, bringing cars and wagons to a skittering halt. Pedestrians took to the high ground as the Brahmans—shoulder humps trembling, dewlaps flapping—lowered their heads, leveled their horns, and charged everything that moved. One cow chased after a flock of black game chickens; the cackling birds dispersed in a thunderhead of dust and feathers. Dogs barked, doors slammed, horns honked. But above all the noise, I could hear our men shouting hoarse maledictions and riding wildly, with horse hoofs clomping noisily over the streets. All the animals were now out of sight.

"I wonder what happened to the rest of them," Grandfather mumbled as we drove through the center of town. "But they've come through here, all right." Some merchants had covered their windows with the thick wooden shutters they usually reserved for revolutions.

"Desgraciadamente, the blacksmith shop has been destroyed!" one Acuña policeman reported. Ruefully, Grandfather inspected the blacksmith's damage: The crazed cows had stampeded straight through his thatch; even the anvil was overturned.

At the international bridge across the Rio Grande, the Mexican customs officers, resplendent in khaki and gold, had tentatively emerged from their office refuge. But on the U. S. side, chaos prevailed. Though the rest of the herd had passed like a sudden storm, one cow remained, standing guard, while American immigration authorities looked out their windows in anger and helplessness.

"We'll just drive on by," said Grandfather. "They don't need to know those cows are ours." He waved and drove on. "I believe that heavy-set customs man was the one who confiscated our garden produce that time." Grandfather was smiling.

But not for long. He had to settle all sorts of damage claims. One cow joined a dairy herd and wouldn't let anyone get close enough to milk the other cows until the sheriff finally shot her.

Even before the first Spanish cow set hoof upon North America proper, the cattle business was a life-and-death matter. At the turn of the 15th century, Spaniards brought their dark, fleet Andalusian cattle to the Caribbean. Turned loose in the islands to roam, the cattle went wild so that men had to hunt them like game.

Hoping to maintain their monopoly, the Caribbean cattlemen invoked the death penalty against anyone selling livestock on the Mexican mainland. Yet neither law nor outlaw deterred a certain Spanish sea captain named Gregorio de Villalobos.

In 1521, he brought six heifers and a young bull from Santo Domingo to Vera Cruz. And so began the great Mexican cattle industry. Soon the conqueror himself, Hernán Cortés, was marking his own cows with a design of three Christian crosses — the first brand on the continent.

An old Castilian tradition held grass to be a gift of nature, so unfenced herds quickly covered the viceroyalty. Beef prices fell. As early as 1538 men complained that the cattle industry had "grown too large for the country."

Sharp-horned Mexican-Andalusians gradually moved north to that part of Coahuila now called Texas. When Anglo-Saxon settlers came to Texas in the 1820's, the Andalusian animals began to breed with North European stock; the mix and the geography produced a formidable beast. As one 19th-century traveler wrote, "the domestic cattle of Texas, miscalled tame, are fifty times more dangerous to footmen than the fiercest buffalo.... Texas was ... an aggressive country. Every bush had its thorn; every animal, reptile, or insect had its horn, tooth, or sting; every male human his revolver.... There is an old army story to the effect that, when General Taylor's little army was on the march from Corpus Christi to Matamoras, a soldier on the flank of the column came upon and fired at a bull.... The bull, undaunted by the numbers of enemies, charged headlong, scattering several regiments like chaff, and finally escaped unhurt, having demoralised and put to flight an army which a few days after covered itself with glory...."

Gen. Zachary Taylor's glory, of course, came with the Mexican War of 1846-48. And the rangy cattle of that frontier were coming to be recognized as Texas Longhorns. Together, man and animal were domesticating each other.

"If the Plains Indian created the mounted Texas Ranger and compelled the Texan to recognize the six-shooter as his own weapon," wrote Walter Prescott Webb, "then the Texas longhorn kept him on horseback and rendered the six-shooter desirable after the Indian had departed."

Webb illustrated his statement with an event from about 1860, when one Texas cowboy needed "to rope a large and powerful steer, with horns long and well set for hooking and sharp as a lance." When roped, the Longhorn "jerked the horse down, and in the fall one leg of the rider was caught beneath him.... The steer ... seeing both horse and rider prostrate on the prairie, turned and with neck bowed, charged upon them. It was an awful moment.... Some persons in such a situation would have been paralyzed.... But not so with the young man: His hand was instantly on his revolver, and drawing it he shot the furious animal through the brain...."

On the Chuparosa, we had a few head of "Longhorn-looking cattle," as Grandfather called them, "but not mean enough to be real Longhorns." They had the angular posture of a rail fence. Usually they were brindle or muddy black and sported a spread of horn three and four feet across. True Longhorns, of course, sometimes wore horns with a spread of seven feet and a surface worn rough with time — "old mossy-horns," as they were called. We kept no bulls of this sort; but the cows, especially those with calves to protect, would sometimes try to hook a worrisome dog or a man on foot. More than once, as some wide-horned cow chased me to the top of the corral fence, I wondered just how mean an authentic Longhorn had to be.

To New Yorkers, who saw their first Longhorns in the 1850's, the rangy animals had "something of a wild look," as reported by the *Tribune*. The *Times* poked fun at them, saying they "would not weigh anything were it not for their horns, which were useful also in preventing them from crawling through fences."

In those days Longhorns were rarely seen in the East. The Dallas *Herald* in 1859 reported a drove of Texas cattle "en route for the North, to feed our abolition neighbors. We hope that southern diet may agree with them."

The diet agreed but briefly, for the Civil War stopped most of the Texas trade in beef. The second beef-producing state, Illinois — crisscrossed by railroads — became the great beef supplier for the Union. In the fall of 1863, poet Walt Whitman watched drovers from Illinois bring a thousand head of cattle through the streets of Washington, D. C. To Whitman the drovers' call fell somewhere "between the cooing of a pigeon and the hoot of an owl."

A high-pitched Rebel yell herded Longhorns a few years later. With peace, Texans returned from the Confederate Army to find and brand their roving cattle. In 1867 the great era of the cattle trails began. By then, perhaps five million Longhorns grazed the Texas ranges. Within the next 15 years another five million head were driven north along the trails, mostly to the Kansas railheads and a new national market for meat. Confederates learned how to move wild Longhorns across deserts and river quicksand, how to fight Indians and hostile homesteaders, and finally how to howl through the big-city temptations of the rowdy railroad cowtowns.

A curious bond grew between the wild cowboy and his untamed cattle. One old-timer told of a stampede scare he had while taking a herd through a town on a Sunday morning. He recalled that "just as we got between two churches, both bells began to ring.... I talked to the cattle as if they were children. They listened a moment and then moved on." By the time that herd got to market, the cattle had formed a close attachment for the trail drivers. Buyers tried to take away bunches of 10 or 20 cattle, but "they could do nothing with them.... I told the butcher to take all the cattle to the same slaughterhouse and to furnish my partner and me each with a horse and we would help him. We got them there without any trouble."

One herd of 3,000 Longhorns might bring a rancher $100,000 — and he could move them for about a dollar a mile. The trail-driving cowboys felt almost as rich when they collected half a year's pay, some $200. Growing out of Reconstruction poverty, the Texas legend began to loom larger than life. As poet Berta Hart Nance wrote, "Other states were carved or born; Texas grew from hide and horn."

But after a booming market in the early 1880's, the Longhorn prosperity faltered. The bony beasts were perfectly adapted to their terrain. They resisted drought and fever tick, but as more railroads made the drives obsolete, buyers turned to the better meat of Shorthorn and Hereford. Within a generation, the pure Longhorn had disappeared. There was "something kingly about him that stirs the blood," wrote a trail driver. "But the longhorn, like the old-time cowboy, is gone...." Today a few selectively bred animals — chosen for build, color, and length of horn — reproduce

E. SIMS, PAT. MAY 30, 1876

H. REYNOLDS NECKTIE, PAT. MAY 14, 1878

GLIDDEN WINNER, PAT. NOV. 24, 1874

BARBED WIRE FROM OLD MEXICO

the Longhorn's looks; but these animals remain simply curiosities. The Angus came from Scotland, and from India came the zebu, a progenitor of the Brahman. And Brahman and Angus combine in the Brangus. Further genetic stirring has developed other breeds, among them the Santa Gertrudis of the King Ranch and the Beefmaster of the Lasater place in Colorado; both boast a high content of Brahman blood.

"I ain't got any use for Brahmas," an old rodeo rider once complained. "I wish they'd left 'em over in India and instead sent us some of them lady dancers. Them Brahmas ain't like other cows.... They're trickier'n a red-headed woman. Other bulls close their eyes when they charge you, so you got a chance to get away. But not a Brahma. He comes a-runnin' starin' you right in the face."

Tom Lasater's viewpoint differs. Though his Beefmasters are a bulky three-way cross of Hereford, Shorthorn, and Brahman, the Brahman seems to have a controlling interest. "Brahmans are a lot smarter than the English breeds," he told me. "You can't *force* them through a gate like a Shorthorn or Angus. You must give a Brahman time to understand. Handled right, they're not mean." Tom proved his point with a herd of Beefmasters — and my 8-year-old son Robert.

"Here, let your boy feed these bulls," said Tom Lasater. He's a persuasive fellow, and Rob was game. Still, it gave me a turn to see my 70-pound son distributing cake to bulls that weighed about one ton each.

At the Snake River Ranch in Wyoming, Ron Willis shakes his head at all the newfangled breeding techniques. "A cow's wants used to be simple," he told me. "She was self-sufficient, had a strong mother instinct. But that's been bred out of them in the last 50 years. Now a cow may be eating hay and she'll walk away from her own calf. It makes my job hard since I've got to keep 'em together."

Last spring I joined Ron and manager Swede Nelson of the Snake River outfit as they moved 380 cows and their 360 calves from Jackson Hole up to their summer grass in the mountains 60 miles away. Perched unfamiliarly on a gelding named John, I realized this was my first cattle drive in more than 30 years. The experience was an odd mix of memory and novelty. I recalled my boyhood days of herding through a dun haze of dust; here we rode in lush grass where even the drag position — behind the herd — was clear and clean. But in some ways, cow behavior seemed immutable.

"We'll leave early," Swede told me. "About 4:30. If you wait till the calves are full, they want to lie down."

Explosion of fence-building that doomed the open range followed the patent of an easily produced barbed wire in 1874 by James Glidden. By 1884 the Government had granted more than 250 patents for widely varying designs. Although fencing often enclosed water holes and blocked cattle trails, it allowed ranchers to keep their herds intact and improve breeds.

"THE 'BOBBED WIRE' BIBLE," JACK GLOVER, 1969

So, before the stars winked off above the Tetons, we began to move the herd out of a dewy meadow. We slapped our chaps and yipped—a sound that carries above all the basso bawling—and the animals coalesced into a herd. Their wet hoofs stirred up swirling clouds of fog. Sturdy cows, feeling the chill, began to jog, their full udders swinging; younger calves toddled in the rear. We entered a fenced lane and the herd slimmed to a linear, thready formation. We slowed down while the animals browsed a bit at the roadside. "By the looks of them clouds, you'll need a good slicker." The words were Ron's; we were walking slowly enough for me to scribble them with notebook propped on the saddle horn:

"Ron dismounts, leads horse, walks limpingly in boots. Chucks rock at a laggard; at another he sicks Penny—his Australian Cattle Dog.... 5:55 a.m. sun explodes over a mountain. Under hoof sage crackles—fresh aroma. Too little breeze even to shake aspen leaves. A cleanliness to all the world."

Rougher terrain—and my horse's jolting gait—interrupted my notes. Our course widened as fences yawned out across the hillsides. At Ron's direction to "fan out and gather them up," I rode through the herd and stayed "about sixty-seventy head from the point." But I was herding more memories than cattle. I'd forgotten, until now, the sheer, blank, bovine stupidity of calves—brains as unsteady as their legs. And I'd forgotten how to look for—and recognize—individual cows.

"Old Freckles has taken the lead again," Swede called. "Freckles is that one." Swede pointed to a part-Hereford with a spotted face. "She walks at a good, steady gait, and she keeps her calf right with her. The whole bunch can amble along just that fast. She led the herd last year."

At noon Swede announced, "We'll stop to let them mother-up." Moving into the static, bawling herd, Swede stirred the cattle like a spoon in a caldron. One wandering cow smelled each disoriented calf; finding her own at last, she licked him, then let him nurse. Gradually, the nervous bawling subsided.

"They're settling down now," Ron said, satisfied. "If they don't find their calves, they'll head back to where they nursed them last.... Well, come on, let's eat. My last meal's wearing a little thin. We'll need to go on soon as the calves've sucked."

So man still moves at his animals' pace. One night a calf was born; and since he was much too wobbly to keep up on foot, he traveled by pickup truck next day.

When the herd bedded down beside a public road, another calf was struck and killed by a motorist. "Have to bring that dead calf with us," Swede said. "Its mother will need to smell it to know its dead. Otherwise, she'll keep going back to try to find it." Half the herd smelled the dead calf next afternoon, bawling and congregating like human mourners—a reminder that cattle have a powerful herd instinct and unite in the face of danger or death. The Hollister Ranch in California, a vast holding pounded by Pacific breakers, once employed the "bloody hide roundup." A beef was killed and skinned and the bloody hide hung in a tree. The smell brought the rest of the herd from miles around. Once gathered, the mourning cattle were ready for cowboys to drive away in a group. Thus the cowman plaits his own behavior with that of his animals.

One night, as the rest of us stretched out on the ground, Ron sipped coffee from a tin cup and let his bedroll lie. I fell asleep at once, and heard nothing until Swede bellowed an order to begin the day.

"Yeah, I slept all right," said Ron. "About midnight I could hear the herd bedding down. Knew they'd sleep good. Of course, sometimes you say that and an hour later you're out of the cattle business."

"Stampede" is perhaps too strong a word for modern-day Herefords, especially for a herd with calves; young ones slow the whole group. But Herefords can run and scatter. And a cowboy can still have his troubles at night. Around the lamplit camp of the Snake River outfit, I thought of other tales and times and of the men who "knew cow." That was the phrase of Ben Borroum, a heroic old trail driver who lived in my own Rio Grande country.

As a boy, my cousin John Hunnicutt lived with the Borroums for a year and a half when John's mother was ill.

"Old Ben wore a Stetson hat with a round crown," John remembers. "Heavy-set, and his legs were bowed—looked like he'd been raised on a horse, all right. He'd go down to the market in the morning before breakfast to get some meat, and usually he'd stop off at the saloon. Sometimes the meat would spoil before old Ben'd get back."

But years earlier, on the Chisholm Trail, Ben Borroum made better time. In fact, in May of 1873, Ben ran up something of a record. With his sidekick, Dunk Choate, he was taking a herd of 2,000 Texas steers to the railroad at Ellsworth, Kansas. They crossed the Red River into Indian Territory without any trouble. "... but the first day after we got across, our lead steer, a gotch-eared old mossy horn, began to snuff," Ben later recalled. "In a few minutes the whole herd began to sull on us.

"We didn't know what to make of it. There was some wind blowing but the day was cool and clear. The boss thought maybe the stuff had got wind of Indians or a panther out in the brush. We bunched them up a bit and got out into open country. . . .

"We hadn't made more than seven miles since sun up, but when we hit a fork of Caddo Creek, about five o'clock in the afternoon, Dunk passed the word that we'd water the critters there, put them on grass and call it a day. . . . They were acting so queer, snuffing and bellering as they grazed, that Dunk told . . . me to stay with them.

He and the rest of the crew went back to the wagon. When our relief came out, he came with them. It was May; the days were still short. The herd began to get down as the light failed. But they didn't get down right. They didn't let the air out of them the way they do when they mean to stay down.

" 'We're going to have trouble,' said Dunk. 'We'll double-guard them till midnight and see how it goes.'

"That old gotch-eared so and so was swinging his head from side to side and not missing a move we made. 'If they make a break, he'll lead it,' said Dunk. 'He's our trouble-maker.' . . .

"I was at the wagon when we heard them go. It didn't take us long to get in the saddle. In a couple of miles, we got them headed and threw them into a mill" — that is, got the herd turned into a circle so it would slow down. "But it was only the beginning. By actual count they busted away twenty-two times that night. They weren't bad runs, but they were runs. I never put in a night like that one. When dawn broke, they were only a couple of miles from where they started. They looked as beat as we did. They weren't interested in grass or anything else.

"Dunk was as mad as he looked. 'All right, boys,' he called out, 'this stuff likes to run and . . . we'll give 'em a bellyfull!' With a wild Texas yell, we charged into them, slapping our coiled ropes in their faces and banging away with our six-guns. But we couldn't budge them; they had had enough running.

"Old gotch-ear had buggered that herd all night long. Time after time, just when we thought we had them quieted, we saw him lead a fresh break. . . . Some of us hadn't finished eating when three bucks and a couple of squaws" — Comanches — "rode into camp. After the usual palavering, they told Dunk they wanted beef. He obliged them. We put a rope on old gotch-ear and took him down to the creek and shot him. Those Indians began butchering him before he quit kicking, lapping up warm blood and filling their gullets with raw meat as they worked."

Authorities agree that most herds quit stampeding after ten miles at most. Still, for sheer terror, few experiences could equal a stampede at night. Teddy Blue Abbott was only 15 when he was helping to hold a herd of 500 in Nebraska one night in 1876. A storm blew up and scattered the herd, and the four cowboys had to ride out wildly over the prairie dog holes to turn the cattle into a mill and gradually slow them down. Next morning one cowboy was missing; the men found his body beside his dead horse. "The horse's ribs was scraped bare of hide," wrote Abbott, "and all the rest of horse and man was mashed into the ground as flat as a pancake. The only thing you could recognize was the handle of his six-shooter. We tried to think the lightning hit him, and that was what we wrote his folks down in Henrietta, Texas. But we couldn't really believe it ourselves. . . . I'm afraid his horse stepped into one of them holes and they both went down before the stampede. We got a shovel — I remember it had a broken handle — and we buried him near by. . . . But the awful part of it was that we had milled them cattle over him all night, not knowing he was there. . . . And after that, orders were given to sing when you were running with a stampede, so the others would know where you were . . . if they didn't hear you they would figure that something had happened. After awhile this grew to be a custom on the range...."

Almost anything could start a stampede if the cattle were jumpy—the rattle of a slicker, the sneeze of a horse, a match struck in the dead of night.

To tire out the herd and get the animals used to trailing, the drivers often set a hard pace for the first three or four days—perhaps 25 or 30 miles a day. Then, with friskiness worn off, men slowed to 15 miles or so a day, depending on terrain. Good drivers, allowing the cattle time to graze as they walked, could actually put weight on the animals during the drive.

The trail boss, a man wise in the ways of cattle and men, fixed the course and pace. He scouted ahead to pick campsites and locate water, and gave his orders to distant riders by sign language learned from the Indians. Since few outfits owned a compass, the trail boss was careful each night to point the tongue of the chuckwagon toward the North Star. That way men could get an accurate start next morning.

Under way, the herd moved at the subtle prodding of two point riders, experienced men who kept the lead animals headed in the right direction. "The main body of the herd trailed along behind the leaders like an army in loose marching order," wrote trail driver Andy Adams, "guarded by outriders, known as swing men, who rode well out from the advancing column ... seeing that none of the herd wandered away or dropped out."

Last, with their scarfs or neck rags masking nose and mouth, came the dust-devouring drag riders pushing, pushing to keep the laggards from being left behind. Sometimes cowboys had to haul a tired, toddling calf across the saddle to keep the herd moving. Occasionally a line rider would trade spots with a drag man to give his friend a lungful of clean air. Otherwise a man had a long time between breaks.

When Andy Adams left Texas on his first big trail drive in 1882, as he recorded in his great novel *Log of a Cowboy,* his boss Jim Flood gave some good advice to the green hands. Over breakfast the morning they left, Flood had this to say:

"Boys, the secret of trailing cattle is never to let your herd know that they are under restraint. Let everything that is done be done voluntarily by the cattle. From the moment you let them off the bed ground in the morning until they are bedded at night, never let a cow take a step, except in the direction of its destination. In this manner you can loaf away the day, and cover from fifteen to twenty miles, and the herd in the mean time will enjoy all the freedom of an open range. Of course, it's long, tiresome hours to the men; but the condition of the herd and saddle stock demands sacrifices on our part.... And I want to caution you younger boys about your horses; there is such a thing as having ten horses in your string, and at the same time being afoot.... Accidents will happen to horses, but don't let it be your fault; keep your saddle blankets dry and clean, for no better word can be spoken of a man than that he is careful of his horses ... in such emergencies as we are liable to meet, we have not a horse to spare, and a man afoot is useless."

The remuda, or herd of saddle horses and pack stock, traveled apart from the cattle, herded by the apprentice horse wrangler. At night the wrangler would usually hold the remuda with hobbles or with an improvised fence of lariats strung together. Only big outfits would have a nighthawk — a man to herd the remuda at night.

Vital to any trail outfit was the chuckwagon, invented by rancher-trailblazer Charles Goodnight. This was a strong wagon covered with canvas. In front it carried food supplies, tools, bedding, and a barrel of water. In the rear stood the chuck box; its hinged door let down onto a folding leg to provide counter space for the cook. Here he kept his tin plates, cups, and ironware. Under the wagon hung a kind of cowhide sling called a cooney, where the cook kept spare sticks or dry cow chips to kindle a campfire on treeless prairies.

Each day started before daylight when the cook yelled, "Come and get it or I'll throw it in the creek!" and the cowboys crawled out of their suggans, or quilts. No one had tents. An old joke was the "Tucson bed," as the boys called it, "made by lying on your stomach and covering that with your back. It was allowable to put your saddle and saddle blanket over your head, should you happen to have such articles with you, as protection from any hailstones larger than hen's eggs."

Breakfast might be sourdough biscuits, beef with gravy, and black coffee. As soon as there was light enough, men got the herd moving — slowly at first, so the cows could graze.

The cook cleaned up, hitched his wagon mules, and struck out toward the noon site five or six miles ahead. He'd have the midday dinner ready when the herd caught up, and the menu would be about like breakfast, plus some potatoes, perhaps, or onions. Other vegetables were scarce. As the afternoon cooled off, the wagon and herd again pushed ahead, maybe seven or eight more miles, before bedding down.

"You sure can spend the night fast with this outfit," a cowboy might complain. And no wonder. The herd had to be watched all night; and if the animals were restless, a man might sleep with his fingers twined around his horse's reins. After long periods of storm and sleeplessness, riders would sometimes smear tobacco juice inside their eyelids; the sting kept them from falling asleep in the saddle.

These were the measures — hardship and danger — that gave the cattle trail its epic Old Testament quality. "Our cattle also shall go with us," says the Book of Exodus 10:26. Many a frontier preacher could quote such Mosaic verse.

Even at the time, men perceived their own heroics, and boys emulated them.

"In a year or two Teddy will be a real cowboy," one trail boss observed when Teddy Blue Abbott was only 14. By his own admission, Teddy that night "growed three inches and gained ten pounds." Like Teddy, a young and recently reunited Nation seemed also to come of age upon the legendary cattle trails.

Most famous of them all in song and folklore was the Chisholm Trail. Not long ago I visited the grave of old Jesse Chisholm, the Scottish-Cherokee wagon driver whose wheels first marked that trade route northward across Indian Territory in 1865. Though Jesse himself never raised cows, he knew the necessity for grass, wood, and water. He took a few cattle up his trail, along with wagonloads of buffalo robes and furs. But his wagon ruts were still fresh when in 1868 Jesse ate some bad bear grease and died, unaware that his name would live in American folklore. Upon Chisholm's

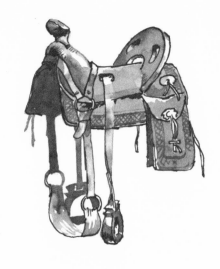

grave on a lonely hill near Geary, Oklahoma, the stone gives a frontiersman's accolade: *Jesse Chisholm... No one left his home cold or hungry....* Aptly, the land around old Jesse has plenty of firewood, grass, and water.

These were attractions praised by the great cattle dealer Joseph G. McCoy in 1867 when he urged Texans to bring their beef animals to Abilene, Kansas, along Chisholm's Trail: "more prairie... more small streams and fewer large ones... fewer flies—no civilized Indian tax or wild Indian disturbances."

McCoy had just built his pens beside the new Kansas Pacific tracks at Abilene. Uncounted cowboys and millions of cattle accepted McCoy's invitation before barbed wire strangled the Chisholm Trail in 1884.

The railroad, though, kept thrusting westward so that every year or so herds were able to aim for a nearer Kansas town: Ellsworth, Wichita, Hays, Dodge City. The cattle route itself gradually shifted to the Western, or Dodge City, Trail.

Nor did all the herds head toward the Kansas railheads. Charles Goodnight and his partner Oliver Loving pushed their cattle through the arid reaches along a vile-tasting creek called the Pecos River, then north to stock the ranches of Colorado. Later, men pushed farther north, to the big cattle center at Ogallala, Nebraska.

And even before Joe McCoy built his Abilene pens, a lucky young miner named Nelson Story cashed in his Montana gold for a thousand Longhorns in Fort Worth. In the wet year of 1866, he pointed them north and crossed Indian Territory without losing a man. But at the Kansas-Missouri border, Story found his path blockaded by grangers and Jayhawkers who feared their own livestock would catch the Texas fever—Texans, in turn, called this tick-derived ailment the Spanish fever. The Jayhawkers, tough guerrilla warriors left over from the Civil War, thought nothing of stampeding Texas cattle and frequently killing cowboys. So Nelson Story weighed the risks and opportunities—and set out west and north for Montana, where gold miners would pay well for beef.

Out of Fort Leavenworth, Story bought wagons, hired bullwhackers, and took the Oregon Trail. At Fort Laramie, Wyoming, the U. S. Cavalry warned him that the Powder River country was aswarm with hostile Sioux Indians. Story drove on, across land where the Sioux had killed 150 whites in six months' time. When Indians stole his stock, he rode after the red men and took the cattle back.

At Fort Phil Kearny, the commanding officer ordered Story to halt and save

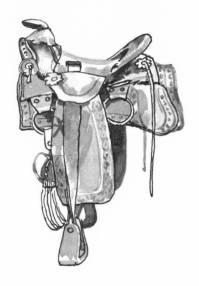

Simple and functional, the working saddle of a Mexican vaquero of 1700, at center, evolved from rigging brought by Spanish explorers; long rawhide tie-downs secured slickers and other gear. Saddles, hand-crafted to individual tastes, eventually became more diversified, with features developed for varying conditions. Tapaderos covered the stirrups on a California saddle of 1870, at left, to protect the rider's feet from heavy brush and cold in northern climates. The wide, form-fitting seat of an 1880 Texas saddle, at right, gave a measure of comfort.

DRAWINGS BY RICHARD SCHLECHT

his party from certain death. Story obediently camped outside the fort; but then, by night, he called his men together, defied orders, and pulled his whole caravan out into Indian country.

Story trailed the herd only at night, but one man had to hunt game for the party ahead of the cattle. Near the Yellowstone River a band of some 15 Indians surprised and killed the lone hunter. Story and his men drove off the raiders, but found their friend's body scalped and riveted to the earth with arrows.

Yet, on Story's whole march, that hunter was the only one to die. "There were only twenty-seven men in our party," one of the men reminisced. "There were about three hundred troopers at Fort Phil Kearny. But the Indians were worse scared of us with our Remingtons than they were of the troopers with their Springfield army guns. After we got 'em scared it was easy for our twenty-seven to stand off three thousand reds with their bows and arrows."

Story, with his herd, finally pulled into Virginia City, Montana, on a chill December day, the first outfit to breach the Powder River Valley and turn a profit.

Oliver Loving had far less luck with the Indians of west Texas. At the moment McCoy was planning his Abilene cattle yards, that soft-spoken Texas trailman, already in his fifties, had just formed a partnership with young Charles Goodnight. Together in 1866 the two men drove a herd across west Texas over a dry area that could claim one waterless 96-mile stretch from the Concho's headwaters to the Pecos. As profit from sales in New Mexico and Colorado, Goodnight packed $12,000 in gold on the back of a mule and returned to Texas.

So the new trail took the two men's names. And Loving's life. It happened the next year in 1867 when "we started another herd west . . . and struck the Pecos the latter part of June," as Goodnight told the story. "After we had gone up the river about one hundred miles it was decided that Mr. Loving should go ahead on horseback in order to reach New Mexico and Colorado in time to bid on the contracts. . . .

"Loving was a man of religious instincts and one of the coolest and bravest I have ever known, but devoid of caution. Since the journey was to be made with a one-man escort I selected Bill Wilson, the clearest-headed man in the outfit, as his companion.

"Knowing the dangers of traveling through an Indian infested country I endeavored to impress on these men the fact that only by traveling by night could they hope to make the trip in safety.

"The first two nights after the journey was begun they followed my instructions. But Loving, who detested night riding, persuaded Wilson that I had been over-cautious and ... proceeded by daylight. Nothing happened until 2 o'clock that after-noon, when Wilson ... sighted Comanches. ... Apparently they were five or six hun-dred strong. The men left the trail and made for the Pecos River which was about four miles to the northwest ... to find shelter. ... One hundred and fifty feet from the bank of the Pecos this bank drops abruptly some one hundred feet. The men scrambled down this bluff and dismounted. They hitched their horses (which the Indians captured at once) and crossed the river where they hid themselves among the sand dunes. ... Meantime the Indians ... surrounded the men. ... The Indians ... speaking in Spanish, begged the men to come out for a consultation. Wilson ... stepped out to see what he could do with them. Loving attempting to guard the rear was fired on. ... He sustained a broken arm and bad wound in the side. The men re-treated to the shelter of the river bank.

"Toward dawn of the next day Loving, believing that he was going to die from the wound in his side, begged Wilson to leave him. ...

"It happened ... down the river, there was a shoal. ... On this shoal an Indian sentinel on horseback was on guard and Wilson knew this. ... and floated noiselessly down the river."

Wilson survived that ordeal, and days of wandering, and finally found Good-night, who nursed him back to health. The men tried unsuccessfully to find Loving's body, then, weeks later, learned from a New Mexico party that Loving had reached Fort Sumner.

Bill Wilson recounted the story this way: "The bullet which had penetrated his side did not prove fatal and the next night after I had left him he got into the river and drifted by the Indians as I had done, crawled out and lay in the weeds all the next day. The following night he made his way to the road ... hoping to find some-body traveling that way. He remained there for five days, being without anything to eat for seven days. Finally some Mexicans came along, and he hired them to take him to Fort Sumner and I believe he would have fully recovered if the doctor at that point had been a competent surgeon. But that doctor had never amputated any limbs and did not want to undertake such work.

"When we heard Mr. Loving was at Fort Sumner, Mr. Goodnight and I hastened there ... Goodnight started a man to Santa Fe after a surgeon. ... But too late. Thus ended the career of one of the best men I ever knew."

Desert crossings, Indian battles, and stampedes represented the most dramatic events on the cattle trails, but probably more lives were actually lost in river cross-ings. A surprising number of cowboys never learned to swim; and even though Longhorns did better than their masters, many cattle still died in the rivers. Ranch-ers in the Cherokee Strip took to calling Longhorns "sea lions"—because "they've done so much swimming on the way up from Texas."

So they had. After crossing the rivers of Texas on the Chisholm Trail, herds then had to cope with the great Red River, the Washita, the Canadian, the North

Canadian, Cimarron (in Spanish, the word means "wild"), Salt Fork, Arkansas, and Little Arkansas. In the early days neither bridge nor ferry could be found on the whole route. Wagons were floated across; all animals swam.

The trick was for point men to crowd the herd compactly and quickly so the lead animals would take the plunge and others would follow. Next came cowboys astride their horses to guide the swimming cattle straight across; one danger was that the herd would turn downstream in the current and become exhausted before reaching the far bank. Often cowboys would ease up on their horses by dismounting and using the horse's tail as a towrope. The cattle sank deep, showing only their tilted heads—nostrils, eyes, and spreading horns. To one trail driver, the scene resembled "a thousand rocking chairs floating on the water."

Flash floods, unexpected currents, and banks of quicksand took a treacherous toll of herds and men.

"The river was on a big rise," trail driver Joe Chapman remembered on one Red River crossing in 1873. "Bill Henson and I were selected to go across and hold the cattle when they reached the opposite side. We were mounted on small paint ponies, and the one I was riding got into some quicksand just under the water and stuck there. I dismounted in water about knee deep, rolled him over and took off my saddle, bridle and leggings, then undressed myself, and called some of the boys to come in and get my things, while I headed my horse for the north bank with just a rope around his neck . . . the little fellow got me safely over. . . . But the herd sulled and refused to take the river, and there I was for twenty-four hours, naked and nothing to eat. The weather was warm and the mosquitoes made a meal off me. When the boys managed to get the herd across next day, my face was so swollen they pretended not to recognize me. They all got a big laugh out of it. . . ."

But laughter was not that common at Red River Station.

"The Station was a good place for a trail boss to weed out his troublemakers and turn them adrift," old Ben Borroum used to say. "If we had any differences to settle, we waited till we got where we was goin'."

The Station also became a center for early traffic jams. Perhaps the worst came in 1871 when some 30 outfits with at least 60,000 cattle waited south of the Red River for a flood to subside. The water "seemed to be a mile wide," said one of the 350 cowboys stranded there, with waves "as white as a wagon sheet." Rain continued to fall; more herds arrived, joining those that had already waited a week. Cattle were soon backed up for 40 miles and scrounging for grass.

The formidable Shanghai Pierce was there, and as young Texas cowboy Mark Withers said, Pierce "was doing a lot of talking, and he wasn't whispering. . . . He wanted everybody to drop back ten to twelve miles, arguing that if a run started, with all the outfits packed in together . . . we would all get hurt—in the pocketbook. . . . but nobody would listen. . . ."

The rain stopped, the sun came out, and a Mexican rider attempted to take his animals across. A submerged log surprised his horse. Tossed into the water, the Mexican tried desperately to grab a steer's tail but missed. A friend went in to save him. Both men drowned with the cattle. So the crowded herds continued to wait.

Two nights later one bunch stampeded. "In no time at all they were all running and milling," Withers said. Brands were hopelessly mixed. "We all had losses that night, some of them pretty heavy. The only way we could unsnarl that mass of cattle was to go to work as though we were on a roundup, everybody cutting out his own stuff and holding it at a safe distance. It took us ten days to get them straightened out. When it came our turn to cross the river, it was a millpond."

Some 125 miles to the west, the Western Trail met the Red River at Doan's Store. In 1882 Andy Adams described the crossing this way:

"The cattle were strung out in trailing manner nearly a mile, and on reaching the river ... we took the water without a halt or even a change of horses. This boundary river ... was a terror to trail drovers, but on our reaching it, it had shallowed down, the flow of water following several small channels.... But the majestic grandeur of the river was apparent on every hand—with its red, bluff banks, the sediment of its red waters marking the timber along its course, while the driftwood, lodged in trees and high on the banks, indicated what might be expected when she became sportive or angry. That she was merciless was evident, for although this crossing had been in use only a year or two when we forded, yet five graves, one of which was less than ten days made, attested her disregard for human life. It can safely be asserted that at this and lower trail crossings on Red River, the lives of more trail men were lost by drowning than on all other rivers together."

A modern traveler must search long and hard to find a living link to the cattle trails. In his 99th year, I talked with old Jack Hart in a California nursing home. "Yes, I went up the trail to Kansas," said Jack; his Cherokee parentage gives him the face of a pharaoh. His voice is clear, but his memory of trail driving is not. "Remember," he says, "those things happened almost a hundred years ago."

But in Calgary, Anna Bruce recalls minute details of her girlhood trip to Canada in a prairie schooner. The year was 1903 when her family gathered their livestock and headed northwest from Nebraska to Alberta.

She remembers the way her mother fed the family: "She'd cook meat and put it in a crock and pour hot lard over it—it would keep indefinitely." Miss Bruce saw Custer's battlefield at the Little Big Horn and "a wagon—a caisson?—with only one wheel ... one of Custer's." She tells of fording rivers ("I was scared to death") and crossing one long desert: "We stopped about 12 o'clock at night and gave the horses a little water. We didn't drink any ourselves." Once her father fell sick "from drinking the water. Mother was careful to boil it, but Dad didn't believe in germs. They didn't think he would live, but he got better."

The dream of Canada lured the Bruces on. Relatives had already arrived and were writing letters "that Canada is just a paradise. Hay is just like a great big fat carpet—and actually that was right. It had never been cut before."

Near Red Deer, they filed on some land. "This was August," Miss Bruce recalls. "So first we had to make up some hay for the winter. And next we made a hay barn. We used it for sleeping because the nights were getting cold. It had a nice clean smell there with the hay. Then we dug a well—got water at 30 feet—and made a log house and homemade furniture. Everybody was so happy. People were all kind to each other."

So the Bruces held to the pioneer priority: providing hay and a barn for the livestock before they had a house for themselves.

The frontier somehow seems more recent in Canada than in the United States. I've never met a veteran of the U. S. covered-wagon era, for example. And certainly the great cattle trails themselves have dimmed beneath contour plowing and four-lane pavement. U. S. Highway 81 almost precisely follows the Chisholm Trail—now running parallel, now covering the very tracks of the herds. Once the Chisholm Trail stretched 600 miles in length, a good 200 yards across—a strip overgrazed, stamped out, eroded by wind and water. Today it's hard to find. Oh, at Rushing Springs, Oklahoma, I drank from a spring that once watered the great trail herds. "Coldest water in town," a 10-year-old boy boasted.

And at the town of Hennessey, a plaque honors "Pat Hennessey, a government freighter . . . massacred, July 4, 1874, by white outlaws masked as Indians." His grave, within a wrought-iron fence, stands two blocks off the main street. Progress has bypassed the old Chisholm Trail.

But the river crossings are another matter. Today spots on the Powder River look the same wide way they did to Nelson Story. Near Girvin, Texas ("There are 13 of us here," said Postmistress Mildred Helmers), Horsehead Crossing on the Pecos presents an arid, utterly unimproved vista of salt cedars, mesquite, and flat-topped hills.

Between Texas and Oklahoma, the Red River remains unbridged at its two most famous crossings. At Red River Station, a junk store posts bulletins about meetings of the Spanish Fort Coon Hunters Association.

"You better not drive down there by the river," one neighbor warned me. "Lots of loose sand. And you can wander around in circles."

I was pleased that the river, red as a wound, retained a little of its chancy past. Nearby I saw oil pumps dipping up and down like large mechanical birds sipping oil from the earth. One sip, I calculated, could have stampeded 10,000 Longhorns.

"Too bad you couldn't have talked to old Mrs. Ross before she died," Winburn Smith told me upriver at Doan's Crossing. "When she was a baby, some hostile Indians came and her family hid out in those trees. Her mother tied a handkerchief across her mouth to keep her from crying. She knew all about the old days."

Mr. Smith, perched on his tractor, was plowing deep in a dry field. On the horizon, two whirlwinds were teetering like tops. "Yeah, worst drought in a hundred years," he said. ". . . Uncle Dan Rogers was another good one, but a bull hooked him and he died. Not many old-timers, not even for our annual picnic in May."

Doan's boasts only a modest plaque to commemorate the millions of cattle and horses that crossed here. But it also displays a 1936 message that reads, "You don't need much monument if the cause is good. It's only these monuments that are for no reason at all that has to be big. . . . Yours, Will Rogers."

3

The Country Belonged to God

"THE CROW COUNTRY is a good country," said the 19th-century Crow Chief Ara-pooish; "the Great Spirit has put it in exactly the right place. It is good for horses — and what is a country without horses? . . . To the north . . . it is too cold and to the south it is too hot. The Crow country is just right. The water is clear and sweet. There are plenty of buffalo, elk, deer, antelope, and mountain sheep. It is the best wintering place in the world. . . . Is it any wonder that the Crows have fought long and hard to defend this country, which we love so much?"

Early white men were less enthusiastic about the good country of Chief Ara-pooish — the region we know today as Montana and Wyoming.

"At first, they didn't know you could keep cattle here in the winter," manager Larry Atkinson told me when I visited the Flag Ranch near Laramie. "Then someone turned out some stock, and when spring came *(Continued on page 103)*

Over high ground golden with balsam root, Res Clute leads packhorses loaded with salt blocks for stock grazing summer pastures in Wyoming's Teton National Forest. He salts ahead of the cattle, luring them to new grass.

"LONG TIME SINCE I THREW THE DIAMOND": COWHANDS THROW A HITCH ON A PACKHORSE.

On the move since sunup, a solitary range rider trails yearling heifers through deep

Montana snow to new pasture on the Powder River, where the herd will feed until spring.

Soldiers out of Fort Sill, Oklahoma, drop hay from a helicopter to stranded cattle. Near Woodward, a rescue team carries groceries toward a snowbound ranchwoman. Residents of hard-hit areas in Oklahoma, Texas, and Kansas call the storm of February 1971 the worst in three decades. Drifts up to 30 feet high left ranch houses isolated and herds without forage. The Army responded by launching airborne Operation Haylift. After a snowfall at the Wyoming Snake River Ranch (below), a wagon driver hauls fodder from headquarters for 270 calves. Even when starving, cattle do not paw through the snow for grass.

Astride Smokey, Ron Willis gets ready to rope a Hereford for treatment of foot rot. Keeping

pace, *his Australian Cattle Dog Penny helps tend Snake River's winter herd of 1,500 head.*

Winter yields to spring below snow-powdered peaks of Wyoming's Teton Range. Herefords

from the Snake River Ranch water at an irrigation ditch during a drive to summer pasture.

Man and beast fight for survival on the hostile frontier. From a snow-covered hill, a hunter signals his partner that a fallen elk guarantees a hearty supper. Below, cows and calves huddle against attack by circling wolves; an old bull makes the snow fly on his way to the rescue. Startled from sleep into action, a camper is instantly ready to trigger shots at an "Early Morning Visitor"—a snarling grizzly.

"If two men were stationed at a camp it was not so bad," noted an observer of life at remote line camps, where cowboys ride the boundaries of their range. Hired by a stockmen's association of four Wyoming ranches, Res Clute and Bob Lucas share routine chores at Fish Creek Cow Camp, their base for tending 2,000 head of breeding stock from June to October. On a foggy morning, 60-year-old Res chops the day's firewood. The log cabin lacks electricity and even radio contact with the nearest town, Jackson, 50 miles away. Vegetables grow in the small corral; other food arrives by packhorse. From a nearby spring, Res gets water for cooking (lower right). By lamplight the partners discuss tomorrow's work: change horses, move 100 cows, pick up stray yearlings. In September, Res will ride the line at a different camp, leaving 19-year-old Bob on his own: "You wonder what the other guy is doing at the other camp, but that's all you do—just wonder."

Saddle-weary at sundown, Bob Lucas washes off sweat and grime in swift-running Fish Creek. Cowboys take a bath "whenever we get a chance." Bob and Blackie, one of 20 saddle and packhorses at the camp, get a noontime break (right) from running bunches of cattle to new open parks in the Teton National Forest; Dingo—part Border Collie—keeps the animals in line during relocation. Forest rangers designate herd areas and enforce grazing restrictions. Stirrup raised out of his way, Res Clute tightens a girth before mounting up (far right).

they were all fat. You see, this grass cures out in the sun, makes its own hay — if the snows don't cover it up. Really puts weight on the cattle."

That discovery — and a booming beef market — once brought hordes of cattle north. In the late 1870's a grass-fattened northwestern beef brought $60 — compared to $50 for a leaner Texas steer. Indian warriors were defeated, and ranchers moved eagerly onto the northern range. The mild winter of 1881-82 recruited more men and stock. A bearded old patriarch — James A. Fergus, in the Judith Basin of Montana — began to warn his neighbors that because "many places are overstocked now" they should raise "large quantities of hay." No one really listened, and a Texas drought brought still more cattle north.

The summer of 1886 was hot and dry. One July day Fort Benton, Montana, logged a record 110.9°, and in North Dakota a plague of grasshoppers devoured the stem-cured grass. Prairie fires left miles of rangeland black and bald.

John Leakey — a Texan six feet six — described the way cowboys battled a Montana grass fire. "I was fighting fire with all my might, whipping it with my old slicker" until midnight. Three days later the fire had scorched 50,000 acres in spite of the labors of some 50 men — "anybody in sight of it." Cowboys killed cattle for use as fire drags — "the biggest critter we could locate in a hurry . . . we skinned out half the carcass and piled dirt on the empty half of the hide. The backbone kept the hide stretched out when we tied our ropes to the front and rear legs and dragged it along the edge of the fire behind our horses."

In such fashion ranchers sweated through the dry summer of 1886. Then fall arrived, and in the Badlands old-timers made dark predictions. The muskrats' fur was unusually heavy, and the beavers were storing twice their normal winter supply of willow brush. Ducks and geese flew south a month early. On the October roundup in the Judith Basin, one cowboy complained that "fools go way up into the Arctic Ocean hunting for the North Pole and it ain't over half a mile from right here."

In November came the first real blizzard, a powdery snow that blew through every crack and nail hole in a house. "As we opened the front door," a North Dakota pioneer remembered, "we were confronted by a solid wall of snow reaching to the eaves of the house." But the worst had not even begun. December seemed no more severe than usual and the new year 1887 started with a January chinook — a warming wind from the southwest. The snow grew soggy.

Then on January 28 the white catastrophe arrived. A Montana rancher estimated that the storm "killed several thousand head of cattle . . . when it is 15 degrees below zero & wind . . . 60 miles per hour."

"My dad got caught in a storm just like that," Mrs. Villa Irvine recalled at her home in Buffalo, Wyoming. "He was out on the Cheyenne River. He got off his horse and crawled in a hollow log and stayed there three days. And my mother — they lived in a little log cabin — she couldn't see out the windows for six weeks."

From the Missouri River to the Sierra Nevada, from Canada to New Mexico and Texas, the winter lay killingly cruel. In the Badlands, sage chickens smothered under the drifts and rabbits suffocated in their burrows. Texas cattle, unaccustomed to such harsh weather, were the first to die. But even acclimated cattle did not attempt to break through the heavy crust of ice. They starved though grass lay just beneath their hoofs. At Medora, North Dakota, they ate tarpaper from the walls of shacks. Near Utica, Montana, they devoured the wool off dead sheep.

Children lost their way between ranch house and stable; some froze to death. Jack Snyder, a neighbor of Dakota rancher Theodore Roosevelt, reported that his partner had died; no pick or shovel could drill through the frozen earth. Snyder had to lay the corpse under the snow and wait for spring before burying his friend.

Roosevelt himself had just married Edith Carow and was honeymooning in Europe. But the grim reports of his cattle losses brought him back across the Atlantic.

Helpless ranchers did what they could. Some cut down cottonwood trees so their horses could browse on the bark and small limbs. Others prodded sluggish cattle off their bedgrounds with pitchforks to get them moving in the bitter cold.

By early February, one ranch manager spelled out his report "... it is so cold that when an anamal lies down their legs freeze.... Cattle are dieing fast." Across the whole northern plains, during all of February, snow fell every day but three.

Near Utica, Montana, in the bunkhouse of the OH ranch, owner Jesse Phelps was struggling to write a letter to a friend, rancher Louie Kaufman in Helena, to "tell him how tough it is."

"I'll make a sketch to go with it," said a young horse wrangler called Kid Russell. Taking some watercolors and a scrap of cardboard from a collar box, Russell painted a picture the size of a postcard. It showed a humped-up cow standing in the snow while wolves circled her. Russell added Kaufman's Bar-R brand to the cow's rump and a title: "Waiting for a Chinook." "Put that in your letter," the kid said.

Phelps looked. "Louie don't need a letter," he said, and mailed off the picture.

"When Kaufman received it in Helena, he got drunk on the strength of the bad news," Kid Russell said later. But the watercolor brought other results. It won wide fame for cowboy-artist Charles M. Russell, as he said, "especially among the cattle-men in Montana who knew about that awful winter."

"And it must have been awful," remarked Bill McGregor when I visited with him near the same OH ranchlands on the Judith River. Bill was born two years after that bad winter, but he heard about those blizzards from the survivors. "You could step from one carcass to the other all along the Judith, they said. Yeah, '86 cleaned out the big outfits here, but it's still awful good stock country. All fenced now. I used to ride all over it. *What?* The last time I rode a horse? About twenty minutes ago!"

"And it still gets 50 below in the Judith Basin," boasted another old hand in Utica's Oxen Yoke Inn. "When it gets that cold," he told me, "you can hear a mouse walking a half mile away."

The blizzard of 1886-87 ended with "a good Chinook blowing" on February 27, as one Utica cowboy recorded. But not until the spring roundups could the ranchers count their losses—anywhere from 40 to 90 percent. The *Laramie Sentinel* reported that one Wyoming outfit lost 11,090 head out of 12,000. Gloom became common. Rancher Henry Jackson wrote a friend who had gone to France for the winter, "No news, except that Dave Brown killed Dick Smith and your wife's hired girl blew her brains out in the kitchen. Everything O.K. here."

Roosevelt visited his own Dakota ranch and called it "a perfect smashup.... The losses are crippling."

Scavengers offered to skin dead cattle for half the proceeds, but by the end of April a Montana dealer wrote, "Bottom is out of the Hide market."

That winter endured too in the hearts of ranch folk. Never again would live-stock be left in winter without any sort of feed. Drive across Wyoming any summer now, and you see men preoccupied with hay. They cut it from highway median strips, and they drag big balers onto the grounds of country clubs. And on ranches a talented irrigation man still enjoys the deep respect of cowboys.

The disastrous winter forced many a rancher and speculator to sell out at any price, trying to recover at least a part of their investments. Cattle were dumped on a declining market, and the beef industry went to ruin.

"Yet, maybe that blizzard didn't wipe out quite as many cattle as the old foremen would have us believe," said rancher Van Irvine, a former president of the Wyoming Stock Growers Association. "You had a lot of absentee ownership then, and a fore-man could blame the weather for his losses. There was a lot of rustling in those days."

No wonder. In 1886, the big Wyoming outfits abolished the biscuit line—the free meals given to the laid-off cowboys during winter months. To cut down on the number of mouths to feed, outfits started charging unemployed cowboys 50 cents a meal. Many an idle man helped himself to beefsteak on the range.

Some of the stealing was big-time, the rustling of whole herds. "Have you seen the Hole-in-the-Wall?" Van asked me. "It's south of Buffalo. Rustlers wintered there." So did bank robber Butch Cassidy and other 14-carat outlaws. The Hole was a valley rimmed by a red cliff with but a single, easily defended breach. There rustlers could fatten their stolen stock while the altered brands healed.

It was a trim, attractive woman named Irene Fischer who told me much about modern rustling. She was working as wagon cook on the Nevada Garvey Ranch.

Now Irene is an unusual woman. Not only can she write poetry and bake a sourdough biscuit "so light it needs holding down," as one man said, but she also styles herself a she-buckaroo. Irene has worked as a fully qualified cowhand with outfits scattered across Nevada, Oregon, and Idaho. "And once I worked for some rustlers," Irene told me one day. "Worked two years—and I even did some rustling for them without ever knowing it. This man and his brother had a ranch, you see, and he told me that some of his stock had strayed over onto another place; now the neighbors wouldn't let him come back onto their land to get his own cows. 'So I'm just going to take 'em back,' he said.

"Well, their system was—they knew a bartender in the hotel. All the buckaroos would come to town, and that bartender would talk to them, find out where the out-fits were riding. He'd pass on this information to my boss. And sometimes he'd get a side of beef for his trouble. Well, my boss knew where he could go to set up a camp on the other outfit's land. Two men to a camp. They'd ride all day and pick up the oreanas—you know, what we call unbranded stock. They'd rope them, tie them down, and then about two o'clock in the morning, their truck would come pick up those oreanas—maybe 20 or 25 head. Haul them to their own ranch. I didn't know about all this until the end. They'd just send me to pick up two or three lost cows. They let me keep one for every three I got back. I had my own brand, so I built up quite a herd—about 55 head. Yeah, all stolen, and I didn't know it.

"Later, I learned my boss had raised all his kids to be rustlers, even the girls. It really spooked me when I found him out. Way it happened was we were at this camp on somebody's land when a plane flew in low. We knew this big ranch had a landing field about 12 miles away. Well, a couple of our riders went down there to see what was going on. And they saw a lot of people—ready to come out and get us.

"We just left the cows and did a cross-country on horseback, and I mean but fast. We made 160 miles in a day and a half—even though a blizzard came up—into a hidden camp in a canyon about 14 miles from my boss's home. A place to lay low.

"It's exciting looking back. You know, we even wore guns. Come to find out, one of these fellows—if we'd actually met somebody—he'd have shot them. That shakes you up.

"Well, when I wised up, I threw my brand away and left my cattle and pulled out. But lately I've heard that family is still stealing. They even steal from each other."

If Irene is the prettiest—and most utterly honest—rustler I've ever met, I can recall others. Like five brothers I knew long ago who still have relatives in Coahuila. The family was large, cruel, and notorious. Everyone knew that the brothers stole cattle, but only two men ever discovered conclusive proof. Those men were found shot dead in a deep pit on the Teniente a year or so before we took over the ranch. I always called that pit Murder Cave, and when the brothers came calling I stared at them with dreadful awe. I can picture them yet: swart, extravagantly mustached, wearing the broad sombrero and tight pants of the Mexican cattleman.

Courteously, through mutual friends, my father warned them to stop rustling our cattle. No accusations, no threats, no challenges. But about then my father began carrying a big black pistol in the door pocket of our Model A. "Be careful whenever they're around," Father warned me. "They wouldn't hurt a child on purpose, but we could have trouble." And then one night, an old man came to our door. He'd run out of gas, he said, and could my father take a can of gasoline and drive him back to his car?

"An ambush!" Mother whispered. "They'll get you away from the house and shoot you. Don't go!"

"We can't refuse help to anyone," Father said. "We'll need help ourselves some day. This old fellow's perfectly safe." There was no use arguing, but Mother is a wily woman.

"If it's safe, then I'll go with you," she said, "in the back seat." Father had boxed himself in.

The rest of the story I got from Mother. "It was terrible," she said. "I was holding that big five-pound flashlight behind that old man so I knew I could hit him over the head if he attacked your father. Well, all of a sudden, he moved over — fast — toward your father. I raised the flashlight to strike, but then he moved back. He made the same gesture several times. And so did I. Later I found out he was just deaf and trying to hear your father talk. Perfectly harmless old fellow. He never knew how close he came to getting brained."

Those notorious brothers didn't give up rustling, but they did practice their trade somewhere else. And they always doffed their hats with deep courtesy when they met my mother. Even without her flashlight.

Rustling is far from a thing of the past. To find out just how much cattle stealing is going on, I talked with Amarillo brand inspector Red Bennett, who can recognize perhaps a thousand brands without looking them up. How much rustling today?

"Quite a bit," he answered. "Just now we've got three boys in jail. But the laws in some states don't help much. Here in Texas our laws were made when it took two days to drive a herd of cattle across a county. Now you give a thief two days and he'll have those animals in Chicago.

"It's hard for us to prove animals are stolen. We find some brands that don't belong with a bunch of cattle. The man just says, 'Well, I sure didn't know that steer was in there.' This year, we've been averaging about three cases a week like that. But a conviction is hard to get. Even with a confession, sometimes.

"Two years ago we caught some boys with 129 stolen cattle. They admitted stealing in six counties, but the district attorneys said we didn't have a case. You just can't get actual witnesses to cattle stealing. And if the truck driver changes his mind and says, 'No, I never stole any cattle,' well, that's that."

Had Red Bennett ever had a shoot-out with rustlers? Red looked a little embarrassed. "Oh, no. It's not like that at all. Only on TV."

George Humphreys has had about the same experience. George worked for the Four Sixes Ranch, headquartered in King County, Texas, for 52 years — and much of that time as manager. But since the whole county even now has only about 500 people, the Sixes always had to provide law and order for everyone. So George Humphreys served as county sheriff and a special officer of the Texas Rangers. His ranger commission was still in force when I talked with him long after his retirement from the ranch.

"No, I never shot any outlaw," George laughs. He's a crusty one, short, tough as mesquite, with eyes as direct as searchlights and a face that seems permanently chapped. He grins without guile. "We never had much cow stealing in this country. Oh, we lost a few, maybe a beef or a calf once in a while. My first case was a boy working for me at a line camp. I thought he was a tiptop boy. Knew his people. Thought a lot of his daddy. This boy'd been working out in Pecos country, and he come back here and hit me for a job.

"Well, I'd just sold some old cows and weaned off their unbranded calves. Big old fall heifer calves, about 400-450 pounds. I thought, 'I'll brand them one of these days when I'm up here.' Meantime they'd be all right in that sod field.

"So one day a good friend of mine — John Brown from Paducah — come down to

see about some bulls, and this boy said he had calves to sell. They even agreed on a price, and then this boy said the calves belonged to a friend of his. Well, John's quite a cow trader and the story didn't sound right, so he dropped by and told me.

"'John,' I said, 'I think you're wrong. I don't think this boy would steal a dog.'

"Then next morning I run into the boy, and he said to me, 'Don't you think I ought to bring in them calves and brand them and put them out in the beef pasture?' When he said that, why that was enough. I knew.

"I said, 'No, leave them for now.' So I see John again and told him to go and buy them calves. Well, John went out and set a time for delivery. The boy said he'd have the calves about 11 that night.

"John told me, so I was waiting for them with two rangers that night, laying down in some crowding pens next to a squeeze chute. It was pretty chilly, too—about the first of December. Well, John drove up in a three-quarter-ton truck with a stock bed on it, and finally the boy come up. They were talking in the headlights of the truck, and the boy said, 'Make the check out to Reilly'—I forget the initials, but it was the name of a man who'd been killed in Jeff Davis County a year or two before. Dead man's name, you see.

"So John handed him the check, and they loaded those calves. When the truck started up, I hollered stop. Well, that boy wheeled around and was running his hand in his coat like he was going after a gun. And one of the rangers said, 'Get that hand out and up high.' He did, too—like to've reached and got the moon. Didn't have a gun on him. I got up on the truck with a flashlight and I knew every calf—by their flesh marks, the condition they were in, and the markings on them.

"I said, 'You know they're Four Sixes cattle, don't you?' And he said, 'Yes, sir. But I want to talk to you, George.' I said, 'No. When you come here, you was broke and wanting a job bad and I put confidence in you. No, you won't talk to me.'

"But I felt sorry for him. First time he'd been caught for anything. So we got him a suspended sentence, about five years' suspended sentence."

Crazed cattle stampede before a prairie fire raging out of control. Ranchers fought the dreaded flames with plowed fire guards, cow-carcass drags, and sodden blankets. As he surveyed a smoldering, blackened range, one old-timer said, "It shore looks like hell with the folks moved out."

WATERCOLOR BY RICHARD SCHLECHT

Thieves didn't always fare so well. Rustling once became such a menace on the old three-million-acre XIT ranch in the Texas Panhandle that ranch hands simply shot all trespassers with no questions asked. Ranchers in the Panhandle are more hospitable now, but one spread still posts a warning: "Trespassers will be shot at and if missed will be prosecuted."

Horse thieves were held in even lower esteem. The reason was simple: In a harsh, waterless land, a horse was essential to a man's survival. Stealing a horse imperiled life itself—and thus the crime became a capital offense.

Franc Shor, a friend who grew up in Dodge City, Kansas, remembers a crippled old beggar there named Jim Hodges. "He couldn't really walk—just shuffle," says Franc. "Hodges had been caught stealing horses, and they'd given him the choice of being hanged or hamstrung." Leniency, Dodge City style.

Along with crime and disputed property rights, other forces worked through the developing West. The Homestead Act of 1862 brought pioneer families with their plows. An Illinois inventor named J. F. Glidden was helping these homesteaders; in November 1874 he patented the first of several sorts of barbed wire.

In Pendleton, Oregon, not long ago, I saw a collector's bottle of quaintly labeled *"Barbed Fence Liniment . . . for Barbed Wire Injuries to Horses and Cattle."*

As a boy, Idahoan Omer Stanford watched some horses encounter a barbed-wire fence for the first time. "They would walk up to a fence," Omer recalls, "and as soon as they touched it with their nose they would strike at it and go right on through . . . badly cut up."

Not all the barbed-wire injuries were so easy to see. One trail driver put it this way: "These fellows . . . the 'bone and sinew of the country,' as politicians call them—have made farms, enclosed pastures, and fenced in water holes until you can't rest; and I say, D--n such bone and sinew! They are the ruin of the country, and have everlastingly, eternally, now and forever destroyed the best grazing-land in the world."

My friend Judge Orland L. Sims, of San Angelo, Texas, recalls fence-cutters in west Texas—"some of the old die-hard open range advocates and small homesteaders." Friends of the Sims family were building fence for a big outfit. "One morning, they went out to the job and found that fence-cutters had cut three miles of fence that had just been completed the day before. Every wire had been cut at every post and some of the posts burned.... Things got so bad that many gunfights ensued."

Sometimes a grudge-bearer set fire to the prairie. "We had trouble with a sheepman once," Judge Sims told me. "And he started six fires on us one July. The fire burned clear to the Colorado River, but it didn't burn too much of us.

"That sheepman—his was a personal grudge. We didn't have sheep and cattle wars around Paint Rock. My father D. E. Sims was the first man to run sheep and cattle together here back in the '80's. Everybody laughed at him, said no self-respecting cow would eat what a sheep had walked over. They were just prejudiced.

"My father never did really like sheep. He liked cattle, but when he went just about broke with cattle he'd go back to the woollies. He remarked many times, though, 'I'd walk a mile to kick an old sheep in the side.' But we didn't have any of those wars between sheepmen and cattlemen."

Still, the early cattlemen showed a certain chill toward sheepmen. I might as well confess it here: My mother's people, the Gists, were sheep raisers. And though this mixed marriage has now lasted well over 50 years, the other Gists and McDowells were never very close. On state occasions, my grandfathers might toast each other in cognac, but they always called each other Mister Gist and Judge.

Stiff formality, of course, was better than buckshot. And plenty of ammunition was used. In Arizona, for example, a feud flared between the Graham family and the Tewksburys, who introduced sheep into the Tonto Basin. Reciprocal shootings brought a five-year score of 26 cattlemen and 6 sheepmen killed.

On the Green River of Wyoming one night, several bands of masked raiders attacked four sheep camps, tied up the herders, and clubbed to death 8,000 sheep. Such were "the sinister bickering and jealousies and hatreds of all frontier communities" that Theodore Roosevelt deplored.

The most famous range war took place in Johnson County, Wyoming. "It's still a touchy subject," a young high-school teacher told me recently in Buffalo. "I have youngsters from both sides in my classes. Feelings run strong." After 80 years.

Old Fred Hesse remembers the war first-hand. I visited him in Buffalo, where he has lived most of his life. "I was six," he told me, "and being the son of a big rancher, I was looked down on. I don't remember how much stock we had, but I do remember punching cattle a hundred miles from home. The other boys were from rustler families—or were rustler sympathizers.

"You see, after the blizzard of '86, some of the big outfits went out of business. They had a lot of cowboys—good ones—and had to let them go. Well, those men weren't going to starve, not with cattle on the range. There was stealing before, but now they organized. Elected their friends to office. In Buffalo you couldn't send a rustler to jail. Things got tough. We moved into town into Grandma Wilkerson's boarding house.

Stalled by a Great Plains blizzard, settlers struggle to free their locomotive from a drift. Expanding railroads began freighting cattle north to market in the 1870's, and within a decade brought the long trail drives to an end.

"Now when the fight took place, two men came by in a buggy to take my mother and us children—four of us—out of town. You see, my father, two uncles, and a cousin were in that battle. We rode all night, got to the Powder River about daylight, and didn't see Buffalo again for two years."

The big ranchers' battle plan was simple and foolish: Two dozen of them and their employees, plus a like number of gunmen hired in Texas, were to seize Buffalo, overthrow the local government, and bring any remaining rustlers to justice. The Texans had all been hired by a detective, Frank Canton, whose own name was an alias. "Most nervous fellow I ever saw," Fred Hesse told me. "I've seen him sit in a rocking chair—afraid to fall asleep. He'd hold a bunch of keys in his hand and put a tin washbasin on the floor. If he dozed off, see, those keys would fall into the basin and wake him up. Nobody was going to surprise Frank Canton."

The war party arrived secretly at Casper, Wyoming, by special train, complete with horses, saddles, guns, and two newspaper reporters. Telegraph lines to Buffalo had been cut. But somehow the expeditioners changed or lost their script. Heading north, they stopped at the KC ranch to besiege two well-known rustlers, Nate Champion and Nick Ray.

While the guns fired outside, Nate wrote these words:

"Me and Nick was getting breakfast when the attack took place. . . . Nick started out and I told him to look out, that I thought there was someone at the stable. . . .

"Nick is shot but not dead yet. He is awful sick. . . .

"They are still shooting and are all around the house. Boys, there is bullets coming in like hail. . . .

"Nick is dead. He died about 9 o'clock. . . . I don't think they intend to let me get away this time."

The siege continued through the day, and Champion continued his notes:

"Boys, I feel pretty lonesome just now. . . .

"Shooting again. I think they will fire the house this time. . . ."

Then, in the words of rancher W. C. "Billy" Irvine, "Champion soon came rushing out, rifle in hand.... He ran into two of our best men, who killed him."

By now, though, the shots had warned the citizens of Buffalo. A posse intercepted the invading cattlemen south of town at the TA Ranch. It was the rustlers' turn to lay siege. The cattlemen holed up in the TA headquarters.

I paced off the battleground on a summer day near where a young girl was grooming her horse. "You can see some bullet holes," she said, pointing to scars on the old barn. I inspected the trenches that the posse used.

"The rustlers would fire on anything that moved," wrote rancher Irvine. The house, he said, "was considerably shot up."

Just as in the Saturday matinee, a U. S. Cavalry contingent interrupted the battle and took custody of the cattlemen. Their protracted trial finally ended with no one going to jail.

Old enmities rankled silently for years. "People just wouldn't talk about the war," Dorothy Mondell Frame told me. "My grandfather owned the TA Ranch then —but neither he nor my father ever told me about that battle."

One of the few objective viewpoints is enjoyed today by Mrs. Villa Irvine, daughter of a rustler and daughter-in-law of a cattle baron.

"My dad wrote a letter about his early life back in 1915," Mrs. Irvine said. She riffled through some neatly filed papers. "Here—'Diamond, Wyo., April 10, 1915.'"

Thus the words of Lee Moore, self-styled rustler and later one of Wyoming's leading ranchers:

"We'll just have to go back to Texas my native state and relate some of the ups and downs I've had in the cattle business. In 1861, when my uncle started to the war of the rebellion, he gave me an old cow and a little calf, and my father gave me a pony and a bridle and a sheepskin for a saddle. At five years of age I was a cattle owner, fully equipped for business. But that winter the old cow died ... and as my calf was not a heifer, my herd did not increase during the war. But when the cruel war was over ... my father added to my uniform a saddle ... and started me out reping"—that is, representing or managing an outfit on a roundup. "Reping in 1866 in Texas was quite different from reping in Wyoming in 1915. We didn't call it 'round-up' in those days. We called it 'cow hunt,' and every man on these cow hunts was a cattle owner just home from the war.... I was the only boy on this cow hunt, and I was looking for cattle that belonged to my father....

"We would corral the cattle every night ... and stand guard around the corral. I didn't stand guard, but I carried brush and corn stalks to make a light for those who were not on guard to play poker by. They played for unbranded cattle. Yearlings at 50 cents a head. So if anyone run out of cattle and had a little money he could get back into the game. For $10 he would get a stack of yearlings....

"Every few days they would divide up and brand and each man take his cattle home.... This cattle hunt continued nearly all summer, and in the winter of '66 I started to school ... two or three days nearly every month when there was any school. When I wasn't going to school, I was picking cotton or cow hunting until

'69. [Then] Father sold his cattle and threw me in with the cattle with the understanding that he would receive $12 a month for my services. So you see I began to slip back. Owner to rep; rep to common waddie" — or cowhand.

Later, when Moore went to work for a rancher named Olive, he found that the outfit "furnished coffee, cornmeal, salt, whiskey, and beef provided you didn't kill one of theirs. We would sometimes get out of coffee or meal or salt, but never out of whiskey or beef."

That beef, which was rustled, brought trouble. "Some unknown parties not in favor of Olive's way of doing business on the night of August 2, 1876, slipped up and set the ranch on fire and shooting began. When the smoke cleared away, I was running across the prairie with my knife and nightclothes and Winchester handed me by a dying Olive. I don't know whether it was loaded or not, but I was afraid to drop it for fear the attacking party would hear it fall. After that I resigned and picked cotton the balance of 1876."

Lee Moore found several other jobs in Wyoming, including one on the Red Bluff Ranch, a place soon bought by Billy Irvine:

"Alas, it wasn't long before we got acquainted with Mr. Irvine. One day Daley, the man who sold the ranch, the boss, cook and myself were quietly eating our dinner in Mr. Irvine's cabin. Mr. Irvine poked a sharp rifle in the door and demanded possession. Mr. Irvine and Daley began to have some warm words and as there was no window in the cabin and that gun was too large for me to pass it in the door I asked Mr. Irvine to please raise it so I could get out under it."

That gunpoint introduction was the first meeting for the two men. On this occasion, Irvine "had our stove thrown out and his put in. And when he left and we were sure he was in Cheyenne we threw his out and put ours back in.... But Irvine finally got the ranch.

"In '89 and '90 I worked for the Ogallala outfit running a wagon when there was any cow work to do. W. C. Irvine was manager. In '91 I established my first cattle ranch.... The laws of Wyoming required a man to brand his calves before they were a year old and as a great many of the cowmen violated that law ... I adopted some of those neglected yearlings and put my brand on them so that cowboys would know whose they were. And also to increase my herd."

Neglected yearlings like those, of course, caused the Johnson County War and the lethal enmity that flared between Lee Moore and his former employer.

Years later that old feud came to a climax in a Douglas, Wyoming, saloon.

"My dad walked in," said Mrs. Irvine, "and there were lots of cowboys in there having drinks. And somebody said, 'Come on, Lee, Billy's buying.'

"Dad walked over to Billy Irvine and said, 'I heard you was going to kill me on sight.' And Grandpa Irvine said, 'I sure as hell was. What are you drinking?' And that was it."

But not quite. In 1909 Lee Moore's oldest son married Billy Irvine's daughter, and in 1918 Villa Moore married Pax Irvine — an ending happy enough for any double feature.

4

Good Water
and Grass

ON MOST MEXICAN RANCHES when I was a boy, vaqueros spent a sweaty part of their time repairing fences. They dug post holes in the stone-hard earth using a crowbar to probe and a tin can to scrape out the dirt.

Since then, manual post-hole diggers have given way to mechanical drills, and fewer hands are needed around a ranch. But actually, the fence itself represented an even greater labor-saving device: When outfits ran cattle on the open range, cowboys served as human fences. At their annual roundups each outfit sent several men to help cut—or sort out—cattle for branding. Thus the roundup was, as one Montana hand called it, "the time when a fellow had to sleep a-running."

In the memento-filled office of rancher Manville Kendrick in Sheridan, Wyoming, I came across a yellowed newspaper clipping that quoted recollections of the famous roundup of 1884: "There were *(Continued on page 135)*

Ready to saddle up, vaquero Jesús Esquivel relaxes for a moment in the tack room at the Luís Hernández ranch near Querétaro, Mexico. Mounted herdsmen riding grasslands from Mexico to Canada all trace their calling to Spain.

"AN OLD NIGHT HAWK LIKE ME": A WRANGLER WATCHES THE HORSE HERD.

Luís Hernández chases an elusive cow back into the herd during a roundup on his ranch in Mexico. Early Spanish cowmen originated both the roundup and the cattle drive. Branding a horse (far left), vaqueros practice the method of stock identification brought from Spain by Hernán Cortés in the 16th century. Left, the vaquero's hard, broad-brimmed hat—worn with strap secured beneath the lower lip—shields him from the sun and protects his head if he falls.

Life on the Pitchfork Ranch in Texas revolves around headquarters—the main house (foreground), bunkhouse (upper right), machine shops, and storage sheds. Unlike many ranches that profit from oil or other minerals, the 163,000-acre Pitchfork deals solely in livestock. On big spreads, two-way radios save time and hard riding. At left, wagon boss Billy George Drennan instructs cowhands miles away. Yet older methods often prevail. At far left, horses tow a truck that tried to cross a sandy dry wash.

Helicopter blades kick up a small Texas twister among mesquite shrubs as an airborne

cowboy bunches strays. The two riders will drive them to branding pens on the Pitchfork.

Shaking out a loop, Jimmy Jack Fields (top) of the Pitchfork moves in to rope a calf. Within minutes a dehorner removes the horns, hypodermic needles inject a healthful vitamin compound and inoculate against blackleg disease, and an iron burns on the brand. Many ranches use a branding table to flip and hold the calves stretched on their sides, but manager Jim Humphreys notes, "Our boys don't cotton much to that." They prefer ropes and a couple of strong backs (right).

Work goes on from "can to can't" for Johnny Hand on the hundred-square-mile Ake Ranch near Datil, New Mexico. When winds fail, a gasoline engine will pump the well at left, one of 14 windmills that water a thousand cattle. With his 2½-year-old son John (upper), he heads for other chores—feeding stock, shoeing a horse. At lower, he works a yearling heifer down a narrow corral called an alley. Expert eyes will quickly judge whether to sell her or keep her for breeding.

Almost swallowed by his hat, "Li'l John" Hand (top) supervises his father's work on a horseshoe at the Ake Ranch. Ready to ride again, Hand leads his horse across the corral. "I started working after school with Mr. Ake's racehorses and just sort of stayed on," he recalls. "I like the outdoors and I like animals. This life gives me both." His Navajo wife Helen (outside their home at right) sometimes helps with the branding. Soon, with aid from the Akes, the Hands will start their own ranch.

Light autumn snowfall reflects day's last light at the Douglas Lake Cattle Company's ranch

in British Columbia. Canada's largest spreads lie in this vast region of open grasslands.

Iron pot of stew and tin cups of strong coffee warm buckaroos at a midmorning lunch (right) on the two-million-acre Nevada Garvey Ranch at Paradise Valley. Below, mustached Nate Morris and his son Clark, armed against the threat of rattlesnakes, heat coffee over a crackling sagebrush fire. An old range tradition calls for testing coffee with a horseshoe — when the shoe floats, the coffee's ready.

Glow from a Coleman lantern illumines faces that mirror the boredom of line-camp life. With faster transportation and easier access to pastureland, most line camps have gone the way of the Longhorn and the thousand-mile cattle drive. This camp, an old homestead called the Little Humboldt Ranch some 40 miles from the headquarters of the Nevada Garvey Ranch, shelters Quarter Circle A buckaroos heading for work in the spring pasture. There they live in tents (left), while watching after 25,000 head of cattle.

about 20 different cattle outfits represented and nearly 200 men with 2,000 saddle horses.... It rounded up and worked 400,000 cattle in six weeks."

For decades, aging cowboy veterans of that '84 operation held reunions to reminisce and brag and renew friendships bonded by the hard adventure. Comradeship—a kind of stag festivity—has always been a part of the roundup. And perhaps the old spirit survives today in its pure historic form only deep inside Mexico.

I have mentioned my friend Luís in Querétaro. "Our roundup"—Luís calls it his *juntar,* literally, gathering—"takes place in the hill country far from comforts. We have only one roundup for branding in the whole year. In January. Cold at night —below freezing. We sleep on straw with a blanket on top, and keep the campfire going—most important, for we drink coffee all the night, sweetened with *piloncillo,* a crude brown sugar. Sometimes we eat chocolate, too, for energy, or live off only things we can hunt. We sleep perhaps five hours. Asleep at 10, up at 2 for our rounds, sleep again a little, then up at 4 to feed and saddle the horses and start counting cattle. Often we sing, for the men bring guitars on their saddles.

"The roundup takes us eight days. The most marvelous days of my life." So says Luís Hernández, Mexican cattleman, gentleman, cowboy.

In at least a hundred ways, old Spanish traditions shaped the cattle customs of the U. S. West. Spain and Portugal were the only countries in Europe to practice cattle ranching as early as the Middle Ages. And their Iberian sons brought their techniques to the New World. Other ideas they adapted.

"At first the Spanish saddle had no horn," explains my friend Dr. José Garreta, a noted surgeon and horseman in Mexico City. "When a man roped a calf, he tied the rope to the hair of the horse's tail. Not satisfactory. So the saddle horn was invented."

In Mexico the horn is a fat, squat post suitable for dally roping; after the animal is caught, it is stopped short when the rope is wrapped around the horn. Texans, on the other hand, generally tie their ropes "hard and fast" around their saddle horns. "Too easy to lose your thumb dally roping," one Texan complained. But I've heard the same words—in Spanish—said about the hard-and-fast technique.

Incidentally, the word "dally" is a bobtailed form of the Spanish *dar la vuelta* — to give a turn. Many other ranch expressions also come from the Spanish: *La reata* — rope—became lariat; *vaquero* turned into buckaroo; *chaparreras* are chaps; *cocinero* —or cook—turned into coosie; *corral* stayed the same, and so on.

But even across the U. S. West, a traveler finds ranch terms varying. The unbranded Texas maverick is called a slick in Wyoming and an oreana (from the Spanish *orejana)* in Nevada. A Texas dogie becomes a bummer in Utah and in British Columbia. The string of saddle horses that Mexicans and Texans both call the remuda, in Montana and the Dakotas becomes a cavvy—from the equally Spanish *caballada.* Far-western Canadians just say "the horses."

Like the words, the paraphernalia takes on regional styles: The Texas saddle horn sits slim and tall and cowboys fasten two cinch straps. The brushy, hilly country of northwest Colorado prescribes a higher saddle cantle to support a rider as he twists and turns. The A-fork Idaho rig uses but one girth and sports a horn stumpy enough for any Mexican — and equally suitable for the dally roping by Idaho buckaroos. And today, as restless cowboys move around, styles are blending.

A U. S. cowboy furnishes his own rig — saddle and bridle and accouterments like girths or cinch straps. At a line camp on the Nevada Garvey Ranch young Dan Fowler complained, "Used to be a rig cost a buckaroo one month's wages, but now it costs more. This Elko saddle," he said while anointing it with butter, "runs $300."

A silver-mounted Spanish spade bit can cost a cowboy $125, and custom-made spurs — with copper-inlay brands of the outfits he's served — can easily cost $40.

Of all his possessions, the cowboy probably takes the greatest pride in his boots — at least Texans do. Black cowboy Bones Hooks noticed this fact when he went to work for the railroad and looked over the men in the chair car.

"You could always tell," said Bones, "if you saw somebody with their boots in the hatrack and their hat on the floor, that they were from Texas."

A yellow slicker, though essential to cowboying, ranks low as an ego prop. Its main purpose is to turn water. Aside from rainy rides, a man may use his slicker to make a tent for fire-building or cigarette-lighting, to flail a prairie fire, or to shoo livestock on the run. But for insulation, the slicker is useless. A Texan named Roy Lowe made the definitive statement about the chill of slickers. After spending a night out in a gulch with only his new slicker for cover, he remarked that "if I had had two slickers I positively know I would have froze to death."

Thus, with his rig and bedroll, a cowboy is ready for business. But the business varies. Around Dickens County, Texas, cowboys boast, "I'm a lover, a fighter, a wild horse rider, and a durned good fixer of windmills."

And there in the big-ranch country where the flat Texas plains tumble off the caprock, many a windmill needs fixing. The Pitchfork has 115 on its 163,000 acres and two full-time repairmen to keep them pumping.

Irrigated with windmill water, a grove of Chinese elms shades the Pitchfork headquarters. Wild turkeys in abundance wander fearlessly around the yard picking at feed that the Forks gives them. With machine shops, barns, houses, and outbuildings, the Forks headquarters resembles a small town; and the cowboy bunkhouse resembles a barracks — on the outside. Inside, the lounge area is carpeted with cigarette butts and splashy stains from snuff spittle. But move into the rooms, and things look better. Each cowboy has a room of his own, complete with a neatly made bed. On the dresser sit pictures of girl friends and rodeo stars and bottles of hair oil. On one man's wall hang several Ace Reid drawings; Ace is a favorite cowboy cartoonist — with a style reminiscent of the great J. R. Williams — who lives on a Kerrville ranch he calls the Draggin' S. His captions run like this: "Shore I'm educated. I've got a Ph.D. — that means Post hole Digger." Or another: "This is shore an unusual spring. We ain't had but two inches of dust."

At the Forks the historic line camps, out near the limits of the range, are gone except for Batch Camp, 16 miles from headquarters. Men used remote line camps not because cowboys are natural hermits, but because they couldn't commute by horse to distant pastures. Cars and roads have solved that problem for most ranches.

On the Pitchfork only Batch Camp remains as a one-man house. A partial dugout, it sits in a gulch beside a windmill and dirt tank. "But the well water tastes nasty and behaves like a purgative," Jim Humphreys remarked, "so we have a cistern, too."

Housekeeping at Batch Camp was explained by Walker Williams, a longtime resident: "If dust blows in one door, I open the other door so's it'll blow back out." Williams was the same cowboy who one year described his observance of Christmas at Batch Camp: "Oh, I looked at the Sears-Roebuck catalogue...."

Actually, Christmas at the Pitchfork is a merry, convivial season. All the cowboys and their families — about 70 people — are invited to a party at the manager's house, and Santa brings presents to the youngsters.

Every March, the Pitchfork pulls out the wagon, as cowboys say. They refer to the traditional chuckwagon, brought out to serve the boys on roundup while they brand, earmark, castrate, inoculate, and otherwise tend the cattle. Since science defeated the blow fly, the rhythm of ranching has changed. When I was a boy no cowboy dared take a knife to a calf in warm months for fear that a fly would lay eggs in the open wound and thus bequeath a squirming mass of its pupae, the deadly screw worm. Inspecting a wormy colt on our ranch one time, Grandfather sighed, "I'd sure sell that one for 15 cents." I looked over the colt — so weak he stumbled at almost every step — and weighed his chances against my allowance.

"For 15 cents, I'll buy him," I said. He survived and grew into a sturdy saddle horse with only a name to remind us of his scrawny past: *Chapul,* grasshopper.

Now, with the screw worm all but gone, cowboys can space out their chores through the year. "Of course," says Jim, "the chuckwagon doesn't follow the herd any more. We sold our mules a year ago."

I suspect that tradition alone keeps the chuckwagon in use. Only half a mile away, a cookhouse, complete with steam tables and cold storage rooms, feeds the rest of the ranch establishment. Yet here, under a canvas tent, the immobile wagon dispenses meals to cowboys who must come to it by truck.

"Yeah, it's hard to get a wagon cook these days," admits Richard J. Bolt, the lanky onetime Baptist preacher who presides here. "The Forks and Four Sixes're about the only outfits left with a real chuckwagon." Richard, or R. J. — no one calls him Dick — began this work at age 8 helping his father, also a chuckwagon coosie. He's justly proud of his son-of-a-gun stew, his sourdough biscuits, and his hotcakes. The cowboys come in for their midday dinner, rattling tin plates and cups, piling them full of stew, steak, potatoes, and biscuits directly off Richard's wood range.

The men sit around on long benches, eating silently. All of them wear their hats. After second helpings, conversation loosens up. Some finish, smoke, grind out their cigarettes in the dirt of the floor. Some take out their pocket knives to whittle bits of wood or shave the calluses off their palms.

As each man gets up to leave, he scrapes his plate, drops it in the washtub, and says, "Thanks, Richard," or "Much obliged, R. J."

Crack horse breaker on the Forks is Jimmy Jack Fields. Since the Pitchfork raises both Thoroughbreds and registered Quarter Horses for its remuda, Jimmy

JA—TEXAS   THREE C'S—ARIZONA   COMPASS A—NEVADA   MATADOR FLYING V—TEXAS

PITCHFORK—TEXAS   DOUBLE X—COAHUILA STATE, MEXICO   FOUR SIXES—TEXAS   XIT—TEXAS

ROCKING CHAIR—TEXAS   THREE CHRISTIAN CROSSES—MEXICO   COW'S HEAD—ARIZONA   DOGIRON—OKLAHOMA

Jack always handles quality colts. He usually starts with 2-year-olds in July, gentling them a bit, and then tying up one foot—generally the left rear.

"He does a good job," says wagon boss Billy George Drennan. "He talks to some of them. And in an hour or two he has them broken. Always tries to avoid bucking. That way they just never learn how to buck."

On the Forks, the cowboys draw for the gentled horses on the basis of seniority. Tradition says that between the shoulder and the hip a horse belongs to the rider; the rest belongs to the ranch. "Beating over the head or spurring in the shoulder means 'time check' [firing]," wrote ranch manager Frank Hastings more than half a century ago. Hastings' outfit, owned by the Swenson family, neighbored the Forks, so his views are still close to those held in the big-ranch country.

"... the love of a horse explains why there are cowboys—not rough riders, or the gun-decorated hero of the moving picture, but earnest, everyday, hardworking boys who will sit twenty-four hours in a saddle and never whimper, but who 'Hate your guts' if you ask them to plow an acre of land or do anything else 'afoot.' ...

"... The horse breaker or 'Bronc Buster' usually names horses as he breaks them; and if the horse has any flesh marks or distinct characteristics, it is apt to come out in the name....

"Red Hell, Tar Baby ... Apron Face, Feathers ... Julius Caesar, Pop Corn ... Snakey ... Jesse James, Buttermilk ... Crawfish, Clabber, Few Brains.... Feminine names are often used, such as Sweetheart, Baby Mine...."

Seeing that name Feathers on Hastings' list reminded me. There's an old sorrel saddle horse on the Forks named Feathers. He is 25, and since the saddle horses on U. S. ranches are always geldings, he can't retire like a Thoroughbred stallion to a stud farm. So Feathers roams around the Forks with a 22-year-old gray. "They're useful," Billy insists defensively. "They run with the yearling mare-colts—hold 'em

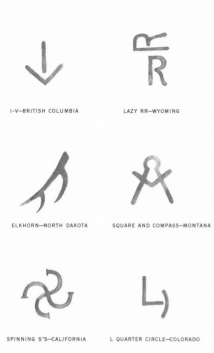

I-V—BRITISH COLUMBIA   LAZY RR—WYOMING

ELKHORN—NORTH DAKOTA   SQUARE AND COMPASS—MONTANA

SPINNING S'S—CALIFORNIA   L QUARTER CIRCLE—COLORADO

Heraldry of the range, cattle brands identify owners and discourage rustlers. Thousands of distinctive irons have seared hides from Mexico to Canada since the 16th century. Representative brands, top row, left to right: Adair-Goodnight; Chiricahua Ranches Company; Nevada Garvey Ranch; Matador Land and Cattle Company; Douglas Lake Cattle Company; Snake River Ranch. Middle row: Pitchfork Land and Cattle Company; author Bart McDowell's family ranch; Four Sixes Ranch; XIT Ranch; Theodore Roosevelt; Poindexter and Orr Livestock Company, first Montana brand. Bottom row: Rocking Chair Ranch; Hernán Cortés, 16th century, first brand in North America; Cabeza de Vaca, 16th-century explorer; Will Rogers; John Bidwell, an early-day Californian; Lasater Ranch.

DRAWINGS BY RICHARD SCHLECHT

together. Besides," adds Billy thoughtfully, "this way they can live out their life."

One dusty day I watched Billy and the other Pitchfork boys load 36 cows onto a stock truck for a 750-mile trip north. "With this drought in Texas, we've got more grass on our Wyoming ranch than here," I was told. The Pitchfork represents one of the few big cattle outfits to stay in the black without any income from oil or other minerals; and one of its special assets is ownership of the 30,000-acre Flag Ranch near Laramie, Wyoming. It's not usually dry both places.

Two months later, I saw the same 36 cows fattened up on Wyoming grass. "Yes," said young Flag manager Larry Atkinson, "we've got about 800 of the Pitchfork cows up here now. It's cheaper to ship 'em than feed 'em down there."

Larry, 6 feet 2 and 200 pounds, is a hereditary cowboy. His dad ranches near Medicine Bow, and Larry has ridden horses since he could walk. Naturally, Larry started his daughter Kim riding at 6 months; his 3-year-old son Shawn, riding alone on a 21-year-old horse, has already moved cattle 20 miles.

These high tablelands shape all the cowboy arts in their own way. Here you find fewer windmillers and more irrigators tapping the streams. And the hardest-working time on the Flag ranch is haying season.

"Carol and I got married just before haying one year," Larry said. "She still kids me. Says I married her just to get a cook for all the extra hands."

"Truth is," Carol said, "two days after the wedding, I was cooking for 17 men."

Since the winter of '86, hayings have mattered more than honeymoons. But modern Wyoming winters bring problems, too. Like the time 800 Hereford cows got their udders sunburned from the reflection off the snow.

"They were so sore," Larry told me, "they wouldn't let the calves suck. We had to tie each cow to a fence post so the calves wouldn't starve."

Larry uses an old Army weasel—a small tracked vehicle—to drag hay out to the cattle in winter. "In January," he said, "we go through all our machinery, to repair it. First week in April, we start on fences — we must have a hundred miles. Then we put about 40 ton of fertilizer on the meadows for our hay.... Finally, the first of May we weigh all the cattle to see how much they've gained during the winter. As the saying goes, we've got nine months' winter and three months' late fall."

To the men on the Nevada Garvey, or Compass A, Larry's job wouldn't be buck-arooing at all. "Around here," said manager Bob Lundgren, "we have buckaroos who never have fixed a fence. All they've done is work from horseback."

That seems like work aplenty. The Compass A, or Quarter Circle A, as it is known locally, owns and leases two million high and dry acres — the Owyhee Desert — a region scored by rocky breaks and brushy ravines. The horizon charts a jagged line of snow-crowned mountains where stock grazes in summer.

"We bring 'em down along September-October," said Walt Fischer, the lanky, angular, acting wagon boss, when I joined his camp on the Little Humboldt River. "Sure, it can snow that early. I've seen it so thick you couldn't see your horse's ears."

The Quarter Circle A wagon is really an oversize truck outfitted with butane cooking range, refrigerator, and big dining table.

"Nobody here calls it chuckwagon," said my Texas friend Curtis Allen. "Just wagon." I'd met Curtis over branding irons one spring at the Pitchfork; now he and another Texan, Jerry Morrison, had rolled into Nevada to see more of the country.

"We'll be going down to Arizona for the winter," added Jerry. "I knew about this outfit from my brother. He broke colts for them once."

So for a while my fellow Texans showed me the ropes. We camped at the Little Humboldt, then moved up to a ravine with rusty cliffs called the Little Owyhee.

Not every buckaroo can be identified here; some give spurious Social Security numbers to protect the privacy of their past. But Mitt McDougall, age 17, has little past to hide. He sprawls on the ground, his head pillowed by a salt block. "I'm plumb out of Copenhagen," he says, referring to his brand of snuff. "You got any ready-mades?" Cigarettes are so called if they don't need rolling. For a while, as twilight deepens outdoors, the boys smoke, whittle, and talk about their last big trip to town.

But then the talk of revels dies down and turns to horses.

"You know Stanford's roan mustang?" asks Earl. "Not bad for a mustang."

"Not worth nothin'," sneers Bill. "Ought to chickenfeed all of 'em." They're discussing the herds of wild horses — not true mustangs by blood — that roam this high desert. Some ranchers hereabouts round up these unclaimed horses for sale to canners as "chickenfeed," or dog food.

Suddenly Walt exclaims, "It's *what?* Nine-*thirty?*" There's genuine alarm at the late hour; 4 comes early here. The lamp goes out. We crawl into our bedrolls. "Seems like a cowboy spends half his life on the *ground,*" grunts Jerry. I overhear a comment, made perhaps for my benefit, about "a man right here killed 76 snakes in this camp all at one time — and all rattlers." But the next thing I know, the shout goes up for breakfast. We crawl out into the cold, dress, and take turns at the washpan outside the wagon. At 4:10, breakfast is an introspective meal.

Someone yodels his coffee. Everyone is polite to the point of muteness. Not even the bumming of cigarettes brings any bantering complaints at this vulnerable time of day. By now, the eastern sky is turning green, but stars still shine as the boys saddle up. Curtis will ride a skittish horse named Charlie Catfish, so he takes no chances: He mounts the dun inside the camp's corral. The horse immediately starts to buck, and Curtis answers every pitch with a jab of his spur. The rodeo goes on for a good ten minutes, until the spur has drawn blood and Charlie Catfish settles down.

"Not a bad horse," drawls Curtis, and his day's work begins.

"The buckaroos out here still do things the old-fashioned way," says Bob Lundgren. "It's like 19th-century ranching." And so it seems. In size, the Nevada Garvey outfit compares with the old three-million-acre XIT ranch in north Texas. The XIT brand, legend says, stood for Ten-in-Texas, accounting for the ten counties its range stretched over. The vast real-estate grant came direct from the state itself in payment to the syndicate that built the Texas Capitol in Austin.

Such are the traditions of the great ranches and their brands. One widely believed story concerns the Four Sixes: It contends that rancher Burk Burnett won his outfit in a poker game when he drew four of a kind — sixes all. Some who knew Burnett deny the story, but it jibes with his personality and luck.

And, certainly, luck has always been essential to the ranchman. "Grass and water were his problems," said Frank Hastings, "and will be . . . for all time."

I thought about luck, water, and grass when I drove out past Ponca City, Oklahoma, past Cow Skin Creek, on my way to the old 101 Ranch. Trader George Miller laid the foundation for this ranch a century ago with ten tons of bacon that he swapped for 400 Longhorns; eventually those animals led to a spread of 100,000 Oklahoma acres. The Millers got on so well with neighboring Indians that they formed a Wild West show as an adjunct to their 101 Ranch.

The 101 show saddle blazes today in an Oklahoma museum, a $10,000 rig aglitter with 166 diamonds, plus sapphires, rubies, and garnets, set into 15 pounds of sterling silver and gold.

Yet Zack Miller died broke, or close to it. The family now owns just three acres of the ranch, including the old 101 commissary. The big white ranch house collapsed in a fire.

A happier kind of story comes from Beryl Rice, whose father Roy Lowe owned a south Texas ranch.

"I've told you about Cy Martin?" Beryl asked me. "Well, he came to spend the night and he stayed 25 years until Daddy passed away. And then ten more years after that. He was company for Daddy. Only thing bad about him was he snored a lot. But Cy was always in a good humor. Never an unkind thing to say.

"People would ask, 'What does he do? Is he a cowboy or a relative?' And Daddy would always say, 'Cy just came to spend the night.'

"We always had lots of company."

And on their Marfa ranch Beryl and John Rice still do. I can vouch for their biscuit line, too, and their hospitality. I'm tempted to give them a 35-year test myself.

5

Come on and Bring the Bunch

ONE EVENING on the Nevada Garvey, I listened to the buckaroos reminiscing about their latest trip to town for a rodeo. Each man tried to outdo the last with a tall tale. I jotted some of their comments in my notebook:

"They advertised 'Street Events,' but that meant fights. More *dirty* fights than I'd ever seen." ... "Every time they'd knock somebody down, they'd kick 'em in the face. About midnight they all started throwing bottles." (Everyone, I noticed, seemed quite unscarred.) "... He had a girl'd make an old cow look pretty. She couldn't fit through that gate." ... "I passed out three times that night. Last time about 12:30." ... "Back in '64 we ate cold watermelon and drank hot whiskey, and talk about *sick*."

And thus the routine of range life, with "nothing new or exciting," as cow trader Joseph G. McCoy noticed, encouraged the off-duty *(Continued on page 155)*

As long as horses or trucks can buck the snows, cowboys with time to spare will ride into town—if only to sit out some of the winter chill. Young Nevada buckaroo Charlie Mariluch idles for a while in Paradise Valley's lone bar.

"WISHING YOU AND YOURS A HAPPY NEW YEAR": EXUBERANT COWBOYS GALLOP INTO TOWN.

"Enter the Law": Strength of the peace officer riding into town shows in his level gaze.

But he had to back up his badge with guns or fists, at least until he earned a reputation.

Crack shots of the Old West line up for a portrait. From left: "Buffalo Bill" Cody, hunter, Indian fighter, showman; "Texas Jack" Omohundro, frontier scout and hunting guide; "Wild Bill" Hickok, who in 1871 secured his fame as a gunfighter while marshal of Abilene, Kansas; "Yellowstone" Kelly, scout for the Army in the Sioux Wars and later an Indian agent.

Wyoming stage of 1904 rattles into Walton, now known as Hiland, in this early example of action photography. Such light carriages, careening behind four horses, hauled mail and passengers on short runs. Teams of as many as six pulled the heavier Concord coaches cross-country, taking about 22 days between Kansas and California.

Mail delivery draws a scattering of cowhands at the Pitchfork post office on a ranch in northwestern Wyoming operated by the "Cowboy Photographer," Charles Belden. Bouncing over rutted dirt tracks, this Model T followed an irregular schedule often dictated by the weather. Even today, mud, flood, or snow can delay ranch deliveries.

"Bull trains," four wagons in tandem drawn by as many as 24 oxen, creak through Miles City, Montana, in 1880. Each train carried up to ten tons of freight from nearby steamboat landings on the Yellowstone River. The whip-popping bullwhacker and his oxen gave way to the railroad here in 1882, when tracks reached Miles City. In 1906 the Bob Saloon (below) in Ismay, Montana, seemed a good place to tilt back a chair and swap news and yarns. Men from the LS Ranch line up at the bar in 1908 at Mike's Place (opposite, below) in Old Tascosa, Texas, virtually a ghost town then. The frontier village had thrived briefly as a cattle crossing on the Canadian River and "Cowboy Capital of the Plains." It began to die in the 1880's as the big ranches ran fence around it and the railroad passed it by.

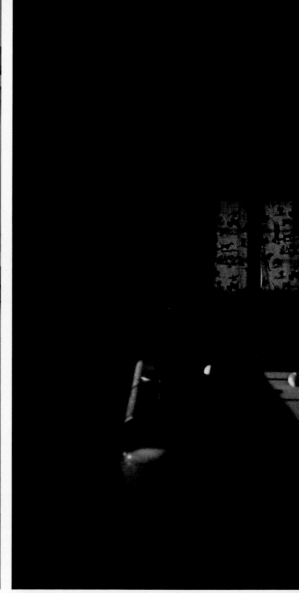

Chance to talk quietly for a time draws men to the
Paris Tavern (above) in Magdalena, New Mexico.
A celebration after the spring rodeo (left) in Augusta,
Montana, might give a cowboy his last moments for
socializing before beginning a summer of work and
isolation. A onetime rodeo rider (above, left) makes
himself comfortable while waiting to buy boots in a
custom shop in Fairfax, Oklahoma. Cowboys prize
fancy leather boots, the more colors the better.

Single pair of ruts marks the main street in Paradise Valley. The unused saloon and hotel

date to the 1880's. A bar and a grocery-gasoline station serve today's few-score residents.

cowboy to "join with some party . . . having a jolly time. Often one or more of them will imbibe too much poison whisky and straightway go on the 'war path.' . . . Many incidents could be told of their crazy freaks; and freaks more villainous than crazy. . . ."

McCoy observed his cowboys in the Kansas cowtowns in the 1860's and '70's. Naturally, decent townsfolk everywhere tried to tame down the rougher element.

Shortly after Motley County was organized in the Texas Panhandle in 1891, my grandfather attended a meeting of its God-fearing citizens. "I wasn't very bashful," he told me half a century later. "They asked whether anyone knew how to handle the legal paper work. I told them my father was a lawyer — that much was true — and that I knew all about legal papers: an outright lie. I was young, of course.

"Well, they made me assistant everything. I'd help the county judge and the clerk. Even made me deputy sheriff.

"So after everybody went home the sheriff came over to me. Name was Joe Beckham, and he was tough. 'Kid,' he said, 'I know you're lying. But I know you're smart and can learn law. And you'd better . . . or I'll kill you.' Meant it, too.

"That's the way I read law — at the point of Joe Beckham's gun. Borrowed books over in Childress, studied for two years at night, and passed my bar exams. Good thing, too. I had to run Beckham's office, and he was away a lot. Turned out he'd stolen county funds and to make up the receipts was holding up trains on weekends 60 miles away. Later he killed a sheriff at Seymour and took off for Indian Territory — a real outlaw. They found his body finally in the tunnel of a dugout; he'd shot it out with somebody."

Another villain was Lee Criswell. "He worked for the Matador Ranch, and those boys all resented it when I locked 'em in jail," Grandfather explained. Once he engaged in a true shoot-out with Criswell: "We both drew and I fired first — shot him through the belly, but the bullet didn't hit his vitals; he weighed about 250. He got well. . . . Next time we met was years later. I was riding and Criswell was leading a pack horse. My heart jumped into my throat. He put his hand on his gun and so did I. We never took our eyes off each other as we passed -- gritting our teeth. Neither of us spoke, and nothing happened.

"And then next time we met was in Dickens. By then, I'd won the livery stable in a poker game. Also the saloon and hotel — yes, son, that was quite a poker game. I owned pretty near all of Dickens.

"Well, Criswell asked to stable his horses, and the livery was all full, so I said, 'You can put your horses up in the stables at my house if you want.' So he did. We got friendly after that. Not bosom pals, but no grudges."

It was that kind of expansive world: win a cowtown in a poker game, do a favor for a man you had shot.

First of the fabled cowtowns was Abilene, Kansas. When Joseph McCoy saw the town in 1867, it was "a very small, dead place, consisting of about one dozen log huts, low, small, rude affairs, four-fifths of which were covered with dirt for roofing. . . ." But McCoy saw that Abilene was "the farthest point east at which a good depot for cattle business could have been made." He ordered pine lumber from Missouri, and in 60 days had pens for 3,000 head of cattle. The great herds followed—along with the "bar-room, the theatre, gambling-room, the bawdy house, the dance house.... [and] those who have fallen low, alas! how low!... In this vortex of dissipation the average cow-boy plunges with great delight...."

If McCoy seems prim, we have the word of a Texan with 40 killings to his debit, one John Wesley Hardin, who in 1871 said, "I have seen many fast towns, but I think Abilene beats them all." And even the mayor's brother once called Abilene "the worst town in America."

Decent citizens had built a stone jailhouse on Texas Street in 1869. Cowboys tore it down. Then the town hired red-headed Tom Smith as marshal. He rode his big gray horse Silverheels down the middle of the street, battered the Texas toughs with his fists, and enforced a new no-gun law—until two Kansas homesteaders murdered him.

As Smith's successor, Abilene chose James Butler Hickok—the legendary "Wild Bill," a natural loner and master of ivory-handled Navy Colts. Wild Bill's career as an Indian scout had already been featured in *Harper's New Monthly*. As peace officer in rowdy Hays City, Kansas, Hickok had pacified a town with 22 saloons and one grocery, where, as a buffalo hunter remarked, "We do not think anything of having one or two dead men on the streets every morning."

Hickok took on Abilene in 1871, the town's busiest cattle season. "Sure glad to see you," Wild Bill would greet the cowboys, "but hand me those guns." One man balked, and Bill killed him. From his headquarters in the Alamo Saloon, Bill presided with his back to the wall. Fortunes changed hands in Abilene that season, but records show not one holdup during Hickok's nine months in office. But Wild Bill made some dangerous enemies.

That autumn, Abilene's *Chronicle* headlined "Attempt To Kill Marshal Hickok" —one of several efforts to collect a rumored reward of $10,000 that a Texas family was said to have pledged to avenge the death of their son at Hickok's hands.

This same rumor followed Hickok north to Deadwood, South Dakota, five years later. "My father rode into town with Wild Bill," Mrs. N. A. Erickson told me outside her mobile home there. "Their caravan came into Deadwood on July 18, 1876. You know what happened on August 2." That was the day reward-hungry Jack McCall shot Wild Bill from behind, killing him instantly. "My father heard those shots," says Mrs. Erickson, "He was just across the street."

I visited the gunman's grave, high on Mount Moriah. Pines scent Wild Bill's resting place, as peaceful now as modern Abilene.

As the railroad builders moved westward, new shipping points took over the Kansas cattle trade. Newton, established in March 1871, had grown into wild decadence by summer. "Here," wrote one visitor, "you may see young girls not over sixteen drinking whiskey, smoking cigars, cursing and swearing...."

On a Sunday morning in August, Newton witnessed the bloodiest shoot-out in the history of the Kansas cowtowns.

The local paper headlined "More Wholesale Butchery" and reported: "The air of Newton is tainted with the hot steam of human blood." The incident then described is still called Newton's General Massacre. In a single exchange between local gamblers and Texas cowboys, nine men were killed or wounded.

Newton faded after one season, and other cowtowns took its place: Wichita, Caldwell, Ellsworth. The Ellsworth *Reporter* estimated 100,000 Longhorns being held around that town alone in June of 1873. About a thousand permanent residents and another thousand floaters — including 75 professional gamblers — swelled the town. Wooden portions of the Drover's Cottage on Main Street had actually been hauled there from Abilene. In addition, Ellsworth boasted a bawdy section called Nauchville and a genuine magnesia-limestone sidewalk 12 feet wide — the only sidewalk on the plains west of Kansas City.

After several nasty shootings, citizens formed a vigilante committee to patrol the streets at night and to run some ugly personalities out of town.

Today in Ellsworth, near the spot where cowboys once nursed their hangovers in the Drover's Cottage, stands a grain elevator for the Farmers Union Co-op — a monument to the nester, the cowboy's heir. But somehow, west of the Smoky Hill River, the Kansas countryside changes character. Trees grow fewer, green fields turn to brown pasture. A marker on U. S. Highway 56 identifies the route as the Santa Fe Trail, used from 1822 until 1872.

The motorist feels that he has reached the West again as he approaches Dodge City. The highway curves, he looks to the left and sees at one glance 30,000 head of cattle. This is a feedlot, a system of pens where a 700-pound steer spends four or five months eating hearty and gaining 400 pounds. Thus Dodge City — self-styled "Queen of the Cowtowns" from 1876 to 1885 — today renews its beefy reputation as a leading cattle-auction market.

"Wednesday is sale day," explains Ford County Judge Camilla Haviland. "The cowboys spend their money celebrating on Wednesday night. So on Thursdays, I may get five or six cowboys on drunk and disorderly charges. . . . But I only handle two or three rustling cases a year. Usually they're sons of Ford County cowboys, ready to start their own herds. We probably don't have more than two dozen real cowboys now in Dodge City itself."

But the cowboy tradition marks every street in town. Some names, of course, bow to television — like Earp Boulevard and Gunsmoke Street. Historic Front Street now carries only one-way traffic, ironically, eastbound. A touristic Boot Hill shows concrete boots peeking from graves of famous old characters. "The original Boot Hill was under that supermarket parking lot," Judge Haviland told me. "And it was moved at least once in the old days."

But if the judge discredits some tales, she savors others. Soon we were talking about Mayor Robert M. Wright and his account of the early days when "Dodge was in the very heart of the buffalo country," and hunters had their wagons "bringing in hides and meat and getting supplies from early morning to late at night."

The town prospered. "A good hunter would make a hundred dollars a day," Mayor Wright noted. "Everyone had money to throw at the birds. There was no

article less than a quarter . . . that was the smallest change. . . . We were entirely without law or order. . . . most differences were settled by rifle or six-shooter. . . ."

So Dodge was tough long before the town inherited the cattle business in 1875.
Mayor Wright claimed that in the first year of the cattle drives, Dodge had 25 killings. Town Marshal Bill Brooks was credited with shooting 15 men in his first 30
days on duty.

Brooks was only one of an all-star roster of peace officers in Dodge City. The
Dodge City *Times* in 1878 called one group of officers "as intrepid a posse as ever
pulled a trigger." They were, too: Sheriff Bat Masterson, Marshal Charlie Basset,
assistants Wyatt Earp and William Tilghman. And the list could have grown longer,
for at other times Bat's brother Ed Masterson, Mysterious Dave Mather, Pat Sughrue, and Tom C. Nixon also wore Dodge City badges.

Those names may explain the advice given by a trail driver when his herd reached
the outskirts of Dodge in 1882. As recorded by cowboy-writer Andy Adams:

"I've been in Dodge every summer since '77, and I can give you boys some
points. Dodge is one town where the average bad man of the West not only finds
his equal, but finds himself badly handicapped. The buffalo hunters and range men
have protested against the iron rule of Dodge's peace officers, and nearly every pro-
test has cost human life. Don't ever get the impression that you can ride your horses
into a saloon, or shoot out the lights in Dodge; it may go somewhere else, but it
don't go there. So I want to warn you to behave yourselves. You can wear your six-
shooters into town, but you'd better leave them at the first place you stop, hotel,
livery, or business house. . . . your six-shooters are no match for Winchesters and
buckshot; and Dodge's officers are as game a set of men as ever faced danger."

But when Andy and the other cowboys reached town, they visited "several
variety theatres, a number of dance halls, and other resorts which, like the wicked,
flourish best under darkness. . . . We entirely neglected the good advice . . . and had
the sensation of hearing lead whistle . . . before we got away from town."

One of the most celebrated shootings there involved Fannie Keenan, alias Dora
Hand, singer at the Alhambra saloon. Because of her unusual beauty and air of

quality, Dora Hand collected conjecture: She came from a fine Eastern family, she had studied music in Europe, and 12 men had lost their lives for love of her. Whatever her real story, Dora's beauty apparently inspired a feud between a Texas cowboy named Jim Kennedy and the owner of the Alhambra, Dog Kelley. The Texan attempted to finish Kelley early one morning by firing several shots into a flimsy two-room shack Kelley owned. But the bar owner was out of town, and one of the bullets struck the sleeping Dora Hand, killing her instantly.

Dora's funeral was the largest ever held in frontier Dodge City. Cowboys, gamblers, businessmen and their wives, dance hall girls, and professional men — the whole town rallied along Front Street to bid her goodbye. And the preacher chose his text carefully: "He that is without sin among you, let him first cast a stone...."

Kennedy's family finally got him off, but neither he nor Kelley ever talked about Dora Hand, who remains a glamorous, mysterious figure in Dodge history.

"Our history keeps cropping up," Judge Haviland remarked. "Take these old coroner reports," she said. "I found them in the basement of the courthouse."

The Judge let me read through the yellowing papers — all of them stories of violent death. One particularly caught my attention: an inquest held on May 14, 1885, "on the dead body of D. Barnes, there lying dead...at the hands of David Mather and Josiah Mather...the said Shooting...feloniously done."

Here I quote from famous Sheriff Pat Sughrue:

"It was Sunday about half-past eight P.M. I dropped into Junctions Saloon, saw quite a crowd in there playing Keno. I saw Dave Mathers and a stranger playing.... The stranger was laughing and talking. Dave beat him the first game and took down a half dollar.... They then played another game & D. Barnes won it. Dave got up & picked up the money & throwed the cards at D. Barnes.... The cards hit him in the breast, scattered on him. The stranger then got up and says, 'This isn't fair. You won my money and I didn't kick about it.... I want that money — it is mine.'

"...Dave...grabbed him & throwed his hand in his breast. I said, 'Hold on — I'll not have none of that.' Dave then let go of him & struck him in the face with his fist.

"Some one hallowed, 'Look out. There is a man pulling a gun.'"

Sughrue scuffled with that armed man, and while he was thus engaged, "the shooting commenced."

Dave Mather's pistol was examined by none other than peace officer Bill Tilghman, who said "two chambers had recently been fired." Barnes was unarmed.

And yet the inquest seems to have had little influence on the career of Mysterious Dave Mather, who also became sheriff in Dodge. The only real loser, at cards and quarrels, seemed to be D. Barnes, deceased.

One recent summer I followed the trail of the Earp brothers west from Dodge City to Cochise County, Arizona, and the notorious town of Tombstone, now advertised as "the town too tough to die."

It was tougher and livelier in 1881. Prospector Ed Schieffelin had named the town for some advice he had ignored: "Instead of a mine, you'll find a tombstone," a friend once warned him. His silver mining claims brought 7,000 people to the community, a newspaper named *The Tombstone Epitaph* and a rival sheet called *The Nugget,* and the usual boomtown delights. To govern them, the town made Virgil Earp city marshal; Virgil's brothers Morgan and Wyatt and their hard-drinking cohort Doc Holliday and the zesty *Epitaph* all rallied round. But Tombstone was riven with another faction: Sheriff John Behan, *The Nugget,* and rancher Ike Clanton's friends the McLaurys — or McLowrys — and Kid Claiborne.

Doc Holliday had been suspected of a stagecoach robbery, and the Clantons had been labeled as rustlers. Historians still argue who the heroes really were on Wednesday, October 26, 1881, at the livery stable known as the O.K. Corral. I confess to a nagging bias in favor of the Clantons, so in fairness I tip the scales the other way with excerpts from the pro-Earp *Epitaph:*

"Three Men Hurled into Eternity in the Duration of a Moment," read the headline. The paper then praised Marshal Virgil Earp and deprecated the "fractious and formerly much dreaded cow-boys." Earp had been warned that Clanton "was thirsting for blood" and had made "threats of shooting him on sight." Earlier in the day, Earp had disarmed and pistol-whipped — "buffaloed" — Clanton and fined him $25 for carrying deadly weapons.

"Close upon the heels of this," said the *Epitaph,* "came the finale, which is best told in the words of R. F. Coleman, who was an eye-witness. . . ."

Here is Coleman's account: "I was in the O.K. Corral at 2:30 p.m., when I saw the two Clantons [Ike and Bill], and the two McLowry boys [Frank and Tom], in earnest conversation across the street. . . . I went up the street and notified Sheriff Behan, and told him it was my opinion they meant trouble. . . . I then went and saw Marshal Virgil Earp, and notified him to the same effect. . . . On reaching Fremont street I saw Virgil Earp, Wyatt Earp, Morgan Earp and Doc Holliday, in the center of the street, all armed. . . . Johnny Behan had just left the cow-boys, after having a conversation with them. . . . when I heard Virg. Earp say, 'Give up your arms, or throw up your arms.' There was some reply made by Frank McLowry, but at the same moment there were two shots fired simultaneously by Doc Holliday and Frank McLowry, when the firing became general, over thirty shots being fired. Tom McLowry fell first, but raised and fired again before he died. Bill Clanton fell next, and raised to fire again when Mr. Fly took his revolver from him. Frank McLowry ran a few rods and fell. Morgan Earp was shot through and fell. Doc Holliday was hit in the left hip, but kept on firing. Virgil Earp was hit in the third or fourth fire in the leg, which staggered him, but he kept up his effective work. Wyatt Earp stood up and fired in rapid succession, as cool as a cucumber, and was not hit. Doc Holliday was as calm as if at target practice, and fired rapidly. After the firing was over Sheriff Behan went up to Wyatt Earp and said, 'I'll have to arrest you.' Wyatt replied, 'I won't be arrested to-day; I am right here and am not going away. You have deceived me; you told me those men were disarmed; I went to disarm them."

The *Epitaph* then editorialized, "The feeling among the best class of our citizens is that the Marshal was entirely justifiable in his efforts to disarm these men. . . ."

A justice of the peace officially agreed, and the Earps have since been exonerated on miles of cinema film. Yet Billy Clanton got a tombstone in Tombstone that reads, "Billy Clanton...Murdered on the Streets...."

Recently, as I walked along those streets, posters in the windows of bars and gift shops read "Welcome Nomads"—a greeting to 500 motorcyclists holding a dance and dinner in town. Leather-jacketed men and their girls roared down the street and patronized the bars. "They're mostly bank clerks," said one shopkeeper. "And those are their wives. We haven't had a fight here in two years." Except, of course, for the bimonthly re-enacted shoot-out at the O.K. Corral.

Does that mean times have changed so greatly? I think not. After water flooded the mines of Tombstone, life settled down. In 1894 Tombstone had a population of just 600—half what the town has today, and less than one-tenth of its boom-time population. Yet it was probably more nearly a typical cowtown in its dull, spore form of 1894, for the average cowboy, wherever he may have been, rarely heard gunshots on his day off. Even a jail sentence was unusual.

Still, I've seen celebrating cowboys ride their horses into a saloon—for example, at the Snag Bar in Red Lodge, Montana, on a Fourth of July. The horses were steadier than their riders, one of whom was so far gone he had forgotten to wear his hat. But those Montana men both fared better than the South Dakota cowboy who rode his horse into a Sioux Indian social with the cry, "I'm General Custer and I'm coming through!" History, I was told, repeated itself almost verbatim.

For the most part, cowboys have quieted down along with changes in the cattle drives, cowtowns, and the marketing of beef. Amarillo now boasts the world's largest single cattle auction company. And though Amarillo may handle $100,000,000 in cattle each year, the city itself seems, maybe, a little less festive than old Chicago.

"Sure, I remember the big days in Chicago—3,000 rail cars here at one time," said Frank M. Flynn in his office at the Union Stock Yard and Transit Company. "Boys would come in on the trains with the livestock. They'd go to the east side of Halstead Street and have a pretty good time. The cowboys might have a few fights among themselves, but we had no trouble with them."

Mr. Flynn talked about Chicago's record year, 1924, when the yards handled 49,000 cattle on one day. "The Prince of Wales came that year and rode around on a horse," said Mr. Flynn. "And in 1954 we slaughtered 'Billy the Billionth'—a Hereford, our billionth animal, they said. Now it's all over. I'm retiring after 32 years. And the stockyards are closing after—how many years?" The Chicago yards opened on Christmas Day, 1865. "Yes, sir, it's been a wonderful place to work—and it's nobody's fault that it's over. The truckers just came in....We lost half a million dollars last year."

I watched Mr. Flynn as he emptied a desk drawer into a sack. I looked out the window at the empty pens. An era was ending in the lusty history of cattle.

"Goodbye, Mr. Flynn," said a secretary. The old gentleman smiled as we went out the door together.

"Yes, wonderful years," said Mr. Flynn.

6
Where Horses and Riders Are Strangers

AS A GANGLY HALF-GROWN YOUNGSTER, my grandfather owned a little mare. "She was a strawberry roan," he recalled. "Pretty. And did I have her trained! I'd go out to the lot, and hold up her bridle and say, 'Come *heah!*' She'd come, too; nuzzle her head up to take the bit. I always fed her by hand.

"And she could run. Fastest thing around Texarkana—that's where I was living at the time. Well, I heard about a matched race coming up north of town. I figured to win me some money. So I put up $25, a lot in those days, and then I bet my saddle. Finally, I even bet that little mare herself. Well, it was a two-horse race. And we finished second.... Sure, it plumb broke my heart. I went home afoot." My grandfather, in his 78th year, laughed as he told me the story—but not so heartily as to explain the tears that stood in his eyes. Since then I've thought of Grandfather's roan mare many a time at rodeos when I've seen a *(Continued on page 195)*

Bronc rider faces his rough-and-tumble moment of truth on the "hurricane deck" at a rodeo in Augusta, Montana. He will get, in the words of Charles M. Russell, "a fine chance to study hoss enatimy from under and over...."

"THE UNDER WAS THE VIEW A TARIPAN GITS": BRONC RIDER HEADS FOR A BONE-JARRING FINISH.

"The cowboy artist," Charles M. Russell (left) takes his adopted son Jack riding at his home in Great Falls, Montana, about 1919. In his "Bronc to Breakfast" (right), an outlaw horse scatters the campfire. A year before he died in 1926, Russell nostalgically painted himself as a young night herder (below, near his horse) in "Laugh Kills Lonesome."

"Waiting for a Chinook": Wolves eye a gaunt cow during the winter of 1886-87, the most devastating ever recorded on the Northern Plains. Unless a chinook— a warm wind—melts the snow, she will starve. Later, someone added the title, "The Last of 5,000." The watercolor gained Russell wide recognition, and in 1892 he quit cowpunching to paint full time.

With a pronghorn buck, jack-rabbits, and a bird or two for Thanksgiving dinner, hunters (left) return to their Montana ranch house. Below, a cowboy races Longhorns stampeded by a thunderstorm. He hopes to turn the herd—force the leaders to veer until all the animals start milling in a circle. Once the cattle have stopped running, he may stay on watch all night, singing to keep them calm.

Buffalo-hide shields and flintlock rifles hang in the New Rochelle, New York, studio of Frederic Remington, painter, author, sculptor, and collector of Western memorabilia. "Without knowing exactly how to do it," he wrote of his first trip west in the 1880's at age 19, "I began to record some facts around me, and the more I looked the more the panorama unfolded." He roamed the West and taught himself to paint before returning to the East to work in 1885.

Grieving father kneels beside the grave of his son, killed on the trail. "...me an Lonnie Fortine tride to cut em back. his horse slipped an fell. Lonnies head hit a rock an killed him dead. we camped an buried him...the boss read some words over him...." Thus wrote a cowhand in an 1893 letter that decades later inspired "The Lord Is My Shepherd." At far left, a cowpuncher's Stetson funnels rain into his lap in "The Good Life." Says the artist, James E. Reynolds (left), "I've loved cowboy lore ever since I was a kid."

Cradling his rifle, Buffalo Bill opens the door of the Overland Mail coach—his rough-riding cowboys have just saved it from Indians. The year, 1903; the place, London's Olympia Stadium. Begun 20 years earlier, Buffalo Bill's Wild West extravaganza gave a blood-and-thunder portrayal of cowboy life. It vaulted sharpshooter Annie Oakley (left) to world fame, and prompted a host of imitators. But the other shows lacked one magic ingredient—William F. Cody, Buffalo Bill himself (above). He caught the attention of the public after a self-styled colonel, E. Z. C. Judson (far left), met him in 1869. Under the pen name of Ned Buntline, Judson made Cody the hero of four flamboyant dime novels, and persuaded him to star in a melodrama in Chicago, "The Scouts of the Prairie."

Vigorous, authentic sketches of the West, where "a man can look farther and see less . . . of anything but land and sky," brought Will James success as a cowboy-artist and author. His books, including Smoky, Lone Cowboy, *and* Big Enough, *describe the open range before the coming of roads, farms, and fences. His 1929 pen-and-ink drawing, "The Mustang Roundup," gives visual form to his words: "I'm kind of sorry now so many were caught, 'cause I have a lot of respect and admiration for the mustang. . . . For they really belong, not to man, but to that country of junipers and sage, of deep arroyos, mesas — and freedom."*

Honors graduate of Harvard University and son of a Philadelphia physician, Owen Wister wrote the first best-selling cowboy novel, The Virginian. *In his many visits to the West, Wister found welcome relief from the stuffy conventions of the East. During his travels, he recorded volumes of observations that gave Old West flavor to his books. The Virginian, published in 1902, told of a Southerner who went west and there embodied the frontier virtues— honesty, strength, shrewdness, and independence. The book's cowboy hero seldom had the time to bother with cattle, but he voiced a memorable command: "When you call me that, smile!"*

Author of some of the world's most enduring Western fiction, Zane Grey works quietly on a shadowed California beach. He began writing as a dentist in New York City, and produced his own first novel in 1904 because no publisher would accept it. After four more years of rejection slips, he took a vacation in the West. It provided him with a new background for his romances, and in 1910 he sold his first manuscript. His next book, Riders of the Purple Sage, had a sale of nearly two million. It began with these vivid words: "A sharp clip-clop of iron-shod hoofs deadened and died away, and clouds of yellow dust drifted from under the cottonwoods out over the sage." He died in 1939, author of 54 books that have sold more than 17 million copies in 20 languages.

William S. Hart in The Aryan, *1916.*

Tom Mix, Claudia Dell, 1932.

Will Rogers plays a cowboy diplomat in the 1924 comedy A Truthful Liar.

Roy Rogers, "King of the Cowboys," and his wonder horse Trigger.

Shadows of wilder days loom large in the Western, most successful movie formula ever. Many stars—including William S. Hart, Will Rogers, and Tom Mix—once worked as cowhands. Roy Rogers found fame as a singing cowboy; Clint Eastwood stars in Italian-made films. Humorist and trick roper Will Rogers liked to say: "I don't make jokes. I just watch the Government and report the facts..."

Clint Eastwood, A Few Dollars More, 1965.

Hollywood continues to invest profitably in the box-office appeal of the old West. Actor John Wayne (opposite) prepares for a scene in Warner Brothers' The Cowboys. On location in 1971 near Santa Fe, New Mexico, a crane-mounted camera (upper) records the action. Playing the chuckwagon cook (lower), Roscoe Lee Browne dispenses food and advice to the trail hands.

During the opening ceremony of a charreada, *Mexican rodeo*, mounted contestants line an arena in Mexico City; at center, the judges wait, poised to signal the start of the performances. In one of a half dozen events, a charro (right) grabs a bull by the tail, throwing him off balance. To gain maximum points, he must yank the animal down and force it to roll over. Most charreada events, like their rodeo counterparts, evolved from range work; Mexicans used this bull-throwing technique to drop animals for branding. Above, a charro's helper holds a wide sombrero.

Arch of sombreros and a cascade of rice from well-wishers mark the end of a traditional charro wedding on the day of a charreada in Mexico City. At the arena, contestant Don Pancho (below) cools off with a popsicle. Young Carlos Ibáñez, a spectator now, has already begun learning to ride and to rope.

G. ALDANA

Grand Entry of the National Finals Rodeo introduces contestants by state in Oklahoma City's State Fair Arena. A cowgirl bearing an American flag (detail, opposite) leads the procession. Arizonan Joe Glenn, 57, world champion team steer roper in 1948 and 1967, waits on horseback (left). The annual National Finals Rodeo offers nearly $100,000 to the top winners in seven events: bareback riding, steer wrestling (bulldogging), team roping, saddle-bronc riding, calf roping, bull riding, and barrel racing — a cloverleaf horse race among barrels for women and girls. Each year, U. S. rodeos draw some 3,000 contestants and 12 million spectators.

Calf ropers compete in an event lasting an average of 10 seconds. "Piggin' string" clenched in his teeth (top), a roper waits in the chutes at Augusta, Montana. With a quick flip (right), a rider at Big Spring, Texas, loops a calf, and another contestant leaps from the saddle (above, center) as his horse stops and the rope tightens. At Augusta, a roper ties the calf's legs with the piggin' string.

National Anthem brings spectators to their feet at the Fourth of July rodeo in
McDermitt, Nevada. Squatting by his gear behind the chutes at Baird, Texas,
rodeo star Larry Mahan works resin into his glove to give him a better grip
for a bareback ride. The All-Around Rodeo Champion for 5 straight years,
Mahan—nicknamed Super Saddle—has earned some $300,000 in 7 years;
in 1969 alone, he won $57,725 for bareback, saddle-bronc, and bull riding.

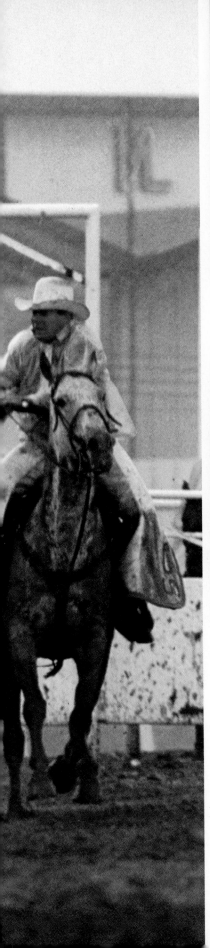

Straddling a pool of mud at the Calgary Stampede in Alberta, a saddle-bronc rider supported by a pickup man slips from his mount after a 10-second ride. A steer wrestler (top) splashes into the quagmire after diving at but missing his quarry, and a mud-splattered contestant quits the arena. Unquestionably rough, rodeos draw criticism from a number of humane organizations on grounds of cruelty to animals. Although enthusiasts maintain that the arena cripples more men than animals, members of humane groups object to roping and wrestling cattle and challenge the use of electric prods and bucking straps belted around the animals' flanks.

With serious eyes belying smiling lips, rodeo clown Wilbur Plaugher
expresses his dual role—to entertain, and to distract bulls from goring
thrown riders. Alert to every move, Buck LeGrande (above) stands ready in
Houston. At Baird, Texas, Tommy Sheffield applies makeup. "With his baggy
britches and barrel-jumpin' antics," wrote one observer, "he's entertainin',
and if he can create a laugh he likes it, but if he's succeeded in savin' some
rider from bein' gored he's satisfied whether he made you laugh or not."

Caught in his rigging at the Calgary Stampede, bareback rider Steve Loney hangs by

an arm as his horse Frankenstein leaps and lunges. He suffered only a twisted wrist.

luckless country boy lose his entry fee, along with his hopes, in the dust of the arena.

It's a young sport, rodeo. In large measure it grew up with county fairs and cowboy celebrations about the time Grandfather raced his little mare, in the last third of the 19th century. But rodeo origins reach much further back. Not long ago I visited with some of the great *charros* of Mexico, those dashing horsemen whose forebears founded the ranching arts in North America.

Watch the grand parade of mounted charros thunder into the *rueda,* the ring, and you see history itself in an extravagant swagger. Fine blooded horses dance in; intelligent and quick, their nostrils aquiver with Arabian and Quarter Horse blood, they seem actively proud of the blazing silver adornments on their tack. The riders wear wide sombreros tilted at a rakish angle; their trousers are tightly fitted, embellished with tooled leather, and accented by the inevitable pistol on the hip. Some of these costumes have cost their owners 100,000 pesos—about $8,000. The charros ride without effort, and the spectator recalls a footnote: Montezuma's Aztec warriors thought the conquistador and his horse were a single centaurlike creature. Here each man-and-horse reconfirms that old confusion.

The horse, after all, gave early Spaniards status and even their name for gentleman: *caballero.* In his North American viceroyalty, a Spanish gentleman lost face if he plowed the earth—but tending cattle from horseback was never considered menial. In the charro's rueda we see no common cowhands. These riders are affluent men who spend their lives plying the noble skills. Like a fencer or foxhunter, the charro enjoys both the dash and the danger. But from Mexico's volcanic soil grows an added earthy quality: The charro must prove and exhibit his *machismo*—his maleness.

So we watch manhood in action with the various events—or *suertes,* as the charros call them: literally, "lucks." And with the *Paso de la Muerte*—the pass of death— luck is a living necessity as riders change horses at full gallop.

Yet the essence of the *charrería* arts is the *suerte de colear,* tailing of bulls. From the long *lienzo,* or passageway, a horseman chases a lanky brindle bull, then catches its tail to twist around his boot, flipping the bull to the ground. "The bull must roll all the way over," says my charro friend Don Rodolfo Goes, "not just flop down."

But in charrería, the tailing of bulls in no way replaces fine roping. The arts of *floreo*—the flowering of ropes—command special balletlike exhibits. And experts with the lasso work afoot to rope ponies neatly by the front legs only.

"We do not race with the stopwatch," says Dr. José Yslas Salazar, president of the National Federation of Charros. "We ride the bronco until it ceases pitching. Unlike your cowboys, we are less concerned with time than with the art."

The word "rodeo," of course, was Spanish for roundup. Historians can document great 16th-century Mexican *rodeos* when ". . . more than 300 horsemen belonging to all the cattle barons" would converge to brand calves—say, "20,000 . . . a paltry number." And in this fashion, the Anglo-Saxon settlers in northern Coahuila learned and adapted a mixture of skills.

A latter-day apprentice was young George Paul. I have known George's family all my life. His grandfather George Miers owned the San Miguel Ranch, the giant neighbor of our own Teniente. I grew up with Mr. Miers's daughter Georgia, and now I was spending an afternoon with her as she showed me her son's scrapbook.

"This is a good picture of him," she said, pointing to one that showed a handsome, dark-haired cowboy with a triumphant beacon of a smile. The headline beside it read, "George Paul Cinches '68 Title!"

"Yes," said Georgia, "that was only his second year as a pro. He was 21—one of the youngest cowboys ever to win the world bull-riding title. Two years earlier, just a week before the finals, he broke his right hand in a fight—yes, he had a hot temper then. Well, he switched to his left hand and still won the junior bareback-riding title.

"It's hard to believe, but when he was little, George was tiny, small-boned. He was 13 or 14 before he started riding with the cowboys on the San Miguel. Then he watched that television show *Stoney Burke,* about rodeoing. Soon he had his own performances out on the ranch, and when he was 16 he went to rodeo school.

"His grandfather didn't want him to rodeo, so George quit it for a year. And it *was* dangerous. He flew his own plane on the rodeo circuit, you know. He was 19 when he crashed one plane—walked away from it. But he had totaled it. There wasn't a pickup load of that plane left.

"Then when he turned 21, his grandfather put George in charge of the whole San Miguel—40,000 cattle, 20,000 sheep, 7,000 horses. He ran it and rodeoed, too.

"I didn't think anything could really hurt George—he seemed indestructible."

His mother turned another page in the scrapbook, and I read the headline, "George Paul, 23, Dies in Plane Crash."

Georgia sat quietly for a moment; her knuckles showed white and she nodded: "It took a mountain to do it."

On the rodeo circuit he is well remembered—in 1970, rodeo cowboys voted one of their number a George Paul Great Guy Award in George's honor.

Rodeo, of course, is only part of the tradition and mythology of the North American cowboy. The legend began to grow after the Civil War when newspapers first reported on the Texas cattle trails and Kansas cowtowns. Joseph G. McCoy and Charlie Siringo wrote their memoirs, and presently the dime novels were coating the cowboy in romance. Buffalo Bill Cody, a scout and Indian fighter rather than a cattleman, then burst upon the scene. With the literary help of an adventurer named Prentiss Ingraham, Buffalo Bill began to reminisce about his life: "But to especially good fortune must I make my acknowledgements, which protected me or preserved my life a hundred times when the very hand of vengeful fate appeared to lower its grasp above my head, and hope seemed a mockery that I had turned my back upon." Such were the sentences crafted by Ingraham. That swashbuckling ghost writer once turned out a novel in a day and a half; a longtime soldier of fortune, he had fought all over Europe and alongside such other warriors as Mexico's Benito Juárez and Buffalo Bill Cody himself.

Cody, ever the activist, did not rest upon his legends. With the organizational skills of an old campaigner, he founded the show that would become famous as Buffalo Bill's Wild West and Congress of Rough Riders of the World. With it he toured all North America and Europe, carrying legions of cowboys, Indians — including, for a time, Chief Sitting Bull himself — horses, wagons, guns, the works.

"The Colonel was the greatest showman of them all..." said Harry Knight, Cody's arena director. "He'd whip off that big white hat and hold it straight out from his side. He wore beautiful hats... He could quiet a crowd like that" — a finger-snap — "when he started to talk.... like the time we played Princeton, New Jersey."

About 250 Princeton students had made some trouble before the matinee and Cody had driven them off "in a kind of whoop-de-doo cavalry charge." But the same students returned to make trouble for the performance that night. When the yelling and pounding started, Cody rode out into the middle of the ring and spoke: "Boys, I want you to shut up. If you don't believe we're serious about putting on this show, just look behind you. A word from me and you're all in one big heap!" The students turned to see a dozen elephants chained to the uprights that propped up the grand-stand. They sat in respectful silence through the whole performance.

"I saw Buffalo Bill's show," old Bob Askin recalled as we talked one evening in South Dakota. "Dad took us down to Sioux Falls. I was about five, I guess. So it must have been 1905. Quite a show they had. I can see Buffalo Bill yet. I thought, Gee whiz! And I guess it got me started."

Start he did, and by the 1920's, Bob Askin — five-feet-eight, 155 pounds — was as famous a bronc rider as rodeo had then produced. But that's ahead of the story.

Meanwhile, back at the ranch, as Buffalo Bill toured the world, rodeo began to acquire its current shape. Pecos, Texas, claims the first big contest in 1883, an organized meeting to settle ranch rivalries. Nobody thought to charge admission. Similar early competitions were held from Miles City, Montana, and Cheyenne, Wyoming, to Prescott, Arizona, and Santa Fe, New Mexico.

The name "rodeo" may date from 1912 when a Western show billed as a round-up opened in Los Angeles. According to Harry Knight, "The... newsboys, mostly Mexican kids, were instructed to whoop and holler to advertise the show... but they couldn't say 'roundup.' So they whooped and hollered '*rodeo*,' Spanish for roundup, and the name stuck."

In the Los Angeles area, and a few other parts, the pronunciation ro-DAY-o seems to survive; everywhere else, the word is universally Anglicized as ROAD-e-o.

In 1913 Oklahoma's Miller family took their 101 Ranch hands into the business of Wild West shows. Soon the 101 Show boasted performances by "the greatest sweat-and-dirt cowhand that ever lived — bar none," as Colonel Zack Miller called Bill Pickett. Pickett was the part-Negro, part-Choctaw cowboy who invented an important rodeo technique.

One day in 1903, on a ranch near Rockdale, Texas, Pickett tangled with a Long-horn steer. Furious at the steer for continuing to bolt the herd, he finally ran his horse alongside the Longhorn, jumped onto its back, and wrenched it down by its horns. As the Longhorn struggled, Pickett bit down on its lower lip and jerked — bringing the animal flat. Soon audiences were paying to see Pickett wrestle steers "like a bulldog," and thus bulldogging grew into a rodeo attraction.

But not before Pickett's sensational appearance in New York's Madison Square Garden in 1905. As Zack Miller told the incident to Fred Gipson, there was a "big old cactus boomer steer with the map of Texas written all over him." As soon as he shot out of the chute, that steer dashed to the arena fence and jumped it, crashing into the grandstand. Fortunately, no one sat in those first rows that night. The steer bolted upward—pursued by the shouting Pickett on a willing horse.

"The crowd was on its feet now, screaming and falling away from both sides of that wild uphill chase," wrote Gipson. "The climbing steer blared like a trumpet. And down at the arena the announcer, fearing a human stampede, lied like a dirty dog.

" 'Keep your seats, folks!' he bawled.... 'There's not the slightest danger.' "

Pickett's hazer—the mounted attendant who helps with bulldogging—was a young part-Cherokee from Oklahoma. He rode right up into the grandstand, too—to the third balcony. Then he roped the steer's heels. Pickett grabbed the head, and the two maneuvered and dragged the steer down into the arena. News photographers memorialized the rescue, and the young hazer was identified as one Will Rogers.

Though this incident in Madison Square Garden was Will's first brush with big-time publicity, he had already performed as a trick roper with Wild West shows as far away as South Africa and Australia.

Will learned the cowboy business on his father's ranch in Oklahoma and driving cattle from the Texas Panhandle to western Kansas—"the prettiest country I ever saw in my life, flat as a beauty contest winners stomach," Will described it years later, "and prairie lakes scattered all over it. And mirages! You could see anything in the world—just ahead of you. I eat out of a chuck wagon and slept on the ground all that spring and summer of '98 and my pay was $30 a month."

His pay increased when he started talking his way through a trick rope routine on the stage. When Will's stunt and his talk came out well, he shared his delight: "Worked that pretty good; made my joke and the trick come out even." Or, if he botched the trick: "I've only got jokes enough for one miss. I've either got to practice roping or learn more jokes." Once he missed an easy trick, tripping as he stepped into a spinning rope. Thereafter he always repeated the error and the comment that brought a big audience response: "Well, got all my feet through but one."

Will Rogers went on to the Ziegfeld Follies, and to vast success as a motion picture actor, columnist, radio commentator, and American folk hero. But with the nostalgia of his countrymen, he looked back to his cowboy beginnings.

"No greater, no happier life in the world than that of the cattle man. I have been on the stage for twenty years and I love it, but do you know, really, at heart, I love ranching. I have always regretted that I didn't live about thirty or forty years earlier, and in the same old country—the Indian Territory. I would have liked to have gotten there ahead of ... the barbed wire fence.... I wish I could have lived my whole life then and drank out of a gourd instead of a paper envelope."

Will Rogers never drew a regular salary from the Millers' 101 Ranch, though he punched cattle there part-time on the Salt Fork range. And it was with Zack Miller that Will first saw a Mexican roper in Buffalo Bill's show, and promised himself, "In

Great Falls
mont
march 12, 1919

Dear Mr Geo. W. Farr I received your kind Invitation to attend the Stock Growers meeting at Miles and I'll be thair with the rest of the reps Cow folks are searce now but I am glade of a chance to meet the few that still live most of my old friends eather rode for or owned cows many of them have crossed the big range but they left tracks in history that the farmer cant plow under good or bad they were regular men and Americas last frontiers men

with thanks and best wishes.
C M Russell

a year from now I'll be doing anything that Mexican did — or wear out every well-rope them Ponca Indians have on the Reservation!"

Nor was Will Rogers the only illustrious alumnus of the 101 Ranch. The live-stock foreman was a Pennsylvania-born veteran of the Spanish-American War named Thomas Edwin Mix. Zack first hired him to wrangle dudes in 1904. Some of the 101 hands had to saddle Tom's horse for him the first time or two, but by 1909, he was handy enough to enter the famous old rodeo at Prescott, Arizona, and win a bronc-riding championship. Thus Tom Mix came to the attention of men some miles farther west who were making motion pictures. He appeared in a film called *Ranch Life in the Great Southwest* — the first of many dozens of silent pictures with titles like *The Wilderness Road, Rough Riding Romance, Night Horseman, The Lone Star Ranger.*

Tom wrote and directed many of his films and selected his own flashy costumes. With such flamboyance, he became America's favorite action star of the 1920's, exceeding even the great William S. Hart in popularity. Then came sound. Tom's voice disappointed the fans, so he again turned full circle in the direction of the old 101 — to the Tom Mix Circus. I remembered it indelibly as only a grade-school youngster could. Tom was parading down Main Street in Del Rio, Texas, astride his famous blaze-faced costar, the horse Tony. I wanted to reach out and touch Tony — but held back: After all, the horse was a Movie Star, and I was only a boy in third grade.

Another young Texan was even more starry-eyed. "As a child in Uvalde, Texas," wrote Frances Octavia Smith, "I used to sit on the bank of the Nueces River and dream that some day I would marry Tom Mix and have six children."

Frances Smith grew up to marry a man named Leonard Slye — but by then she had changed her name to Dale Evans and he was known as Roy Rogers. "As it turned out," Dale remarks today, "I came pretty close to my dream, didn't I?"

Roy Rogers is another grown-up Tom Mix fan, an Ohio farm boy from "way back in the hills," as he told me on his Apple Valley ranch one California afternoon. "I started riding horses when I was seven. Before that I rode mules. And I learned to play the guitar from my mother and dad. They played for the square dances."

In 1930 the Slyes drove west in an ancient Dodge sedan. "Our car broke down near Magdalena, New Mexico—in the middle of nowhere—so we had to hitchhike into town. Well, an old boy picked us up, and he was a cowboy who'd been to a square dance all night. That was the first cowboy I ever met."

A music-loving cowboy made an apt introduction for the lad. For in a few years, Roy was singing with an enormously popular vocal group, the Sons of the Pioneers.

"In 1935 we were playing a benefit for the Salvation Army in San Bernardino, California," Roy remembers today. "Will Rogers was the star of the show—he was everybody's favorite—and he had a friend with him, Wiley Post. They were all excited about this plane they'd fixed up, and they were going to Alaska. I'd met Will Rogers before, but that was the first time I ever really got to talk with him. Next day he and Post left for Alaska. And when everybody heard about their plane crash near Point Barrow, it really stopped the world.

"I said if I ever had the chance to go there, I would." Roy finally got his chance— some 25 years later. "We landed right where they have a monument now. Will Rogers wasn't only a great humorist, he was a great person." Thus paths crisscross in a wide Western world that also seems curiously small and neighborly.

Roy Rogers went on to star in 87 feature films, a host of television shows, some 5,000 charitable appearances, and even comic strips with a weekly circulation of 63 million. At age 59, Roy began a new career: recording country-Western music as a soloist—and promptly bubbled high up the sales charts.

J. Frank Dobie took a squinting glimpse at the sentimentality of many cowboy ballads: They were "frequently wailing through calf slobber." But not always.

Take the experience of folklorist John A. Lomax, who in 1908 found a Negro singer and chuckwagon cook "leaning against a stunted mulberry tree at the rear of his place of business, a low drinking dive" in San Antonio, Texas. As Lomax recalled, "... among other songs he gave me the words and tune of 'Home on the Range.' Both the words and the tune sung today were first printed in the 1910 edition of *Cowboy Songs,* and attracted no attention for nearly twenty years. Then two sheet-music arrangements—one pirated—helped the tune to a radio audience...."

And so it goes: rodeo, Western movies, country music—no one can now draw a firm line between the cowboy and show business. Any visitor to the National Cowboy Hall of Fame in Oklahoma City can see how closely the arts have fused.

The legendary Casey Tibbs is another case in point. This South Dakota cowboy and rodeo superstar of the 1950's today plays bit parts and produces motion pictures.

"Yeah, in this picture *The Cowboys,*" he explains, "my speaking part is like one-liners. I say, 'They went thataway.' But producing films has a greater challenge. It's interesting to see an idea come to life," he told me in his Hollywood apartment.

But films haven't really taken the country out of the boy. During the 1970 Los

Angeles earthquake Casey got an earth-shaking idea. He already owned 400 tough, unbroken horses on some Sioux Indian Reservation lands near Pierre, South Dakota. Why not recruit paying guests to help him round up those wild horses?

So, while Casey played Tom Sawyer, I watched several dozen prosperous horse fanciers help him paint his fence. With his Irish cunning, Casey had other projects going: Advertising people were taking pictures for Marlboro cigarette ads, a Canadian motion-picture crew was filming the roundup itself—and so on. At the epicenter of everything was the engaging Casey Tibbs, long of charm, short of temper, ever quick and quotable. Ride a bronc? "You just fall into the rhythm and it's like dancing with a girl.... But you've got to know your business. If not, you'll either pop your gizzard or eat dirt."

An evening campfire brings mellow autobiography: "Yes, I was one of ten children. I was supposed to be born in a hospital, but the weather was bad, so I was born in a dugout like seven others of us.... Did I ever show you pictures of our old log house? Well, Bart, it was so bad that when they put in a dam there, they had to whitewash the place before they could condemn it. I'm just kidding. When I was a boy, I thought it was the biggest place in the county...

"The *toughest* event in rodeo? Well, what's tough for one person is easy for somebody else. But saddle-bronc riding is the classic event. You need coordination, balance, timing. Now bull riding—while it looks tougher—is easiest to qualify in; a guy might come out of a city and ride bulls. Roping is just a matter of skill....

"I remember old Homer Pettigrew, a top steer wrestler in the '40's; as he got older, he'd say, 'They don't have fun at rodeos like they used to.' And I'd say, 'Yeah, Homer, it's just a different bunch of guys that's having the fun.' Well, maybe. But it's more a dog-eat-dog business now. We'd always try to get up north to Pendleton and Lewiston a few days ahead of time and stay a few days later. Same way to Calgary. Now you've got to leave within 30 minutes to get to another rodeo."

Among the different guys having the fun are Marty Wood, three times world saddle-bronc champion, a tough, moody Canadian who jokingly boasts, "I train on whiskey and water." Wood's occasional brawls have had more publicity than, say, the clear-eyed sobriety of Shawn Davis, also a three-time saddle-bronc champion.

The son of a Montana rancher, Shawn is a Mormon convert who tithes his winnings and neither drinks nor smokes. Shawn's bland good looks conceal his hardiness. "He's got lots of grit in his craw," one colleague assured me at a rodeo in Big Spring, Texas. "Ask Shawn about his accident."

"Oh, that," he said. "Well, it happened in Thompson Falls, Montana. I'd flown all night in my own plane to get there, and I was bareback riding. It was a normal buck, then the horse just went over backwards—1,100 pounds on my shoulders. Broke my back. Well, they put me in the ambulance—and slammed the door on my hands. Then the ambulance ran out of gas. I was five hours getting to the hospital." Doctors operated, fusing the broken vertebrae, but said Shawn would never ride again. "They thought I'd always drag my right leg," he told me. "But I did my exercises—so one year and one month after that accident, I went to Jim Shoulders'

CMR 1907

I wonder what's the matter with them fool hosses?

I aint wonderin'! from looks them hosses is wise.

Sun shine and shadow

Rodeo Riding School. You know Jim Shoulders. He took 16 world rodeo championships before he hung up his rigging. Well, I got on a bronc—and it didn't hurt at all. Loosened me up. Next day I tried again, and got more confidence. Then I entered a rodeo at Gladewater, Texas. Made 69 points. Next night at Beaumont I won third. Remember—saddle-bronc riding doesn't take the strength of bareback. More balance and timing.

"Of course, now if I sit around a week, I can't get around. So I stay with it."

Later I watched Shawn Davis stay with it on a saddle bronc. He finished out of the money, but he was grinning as he hefted his saddle toward a plane for the next rodeo. A half ton of horse might break Shawn's back, but not his spirit.

Every rodeo contestant has his own special story. Gary Leffew, for example, couldn't ride a horse at all. "I spent all my time in pool halls and riding in a hot rod with a revved-up engine. Then after high school I turned to wilder things—an early commune. Had a big beard and long hair. Then one night I was in Clovis, California, when they were having a rodeo and I'd been in this fight with a cowboy—and I'd won. So next day I went by the rodeo and looked at one of those bulls, and said, 'I bet I could ride that son of a buck.' And those cowboys said, 'Yeah, sure.' They couldn't wait to put a pair of boots on me. Well, they set me down on that bull in the chute. Man, he was a-fighting and a-stomping and a-blowing. Well, I grabbed hold and out we went. He slung me around for a while, and then he threw me 20 feet. I hit rolling. But I said, 'That's fun.' Kind of surprised those cowboys." In 1970 Gary won the bull-riding championship. Now he's clean-shaven, wears his hair short, and still has some trouble riding a horse.

Black cowboy Wayne Orme once had a tough choice: "I turned down a West Point appointment to go rodeoing," he told me in Pendleton, Oregon. Had he any regrets? "No, I went on to get a degree in business administration at UCLA. So I have a job now with a title insurance company along with this rodeoing."

Wayne's parents had 13 children and little money, so at age 9 Wayne was farmed out to a physician who owned a ranch. "I learned to ride a horse then," Wayne recalled. "And I pestered the cowboys to show me how to ride bucking ponies and rope calves. Then when I was 11, they had a kind of junior rodeo there, roping baby calves and all—and I won $4.08. Bought my first pair of jeans....

"Rodeo's a kind of rough life. I've been in the hospital 11 times and had two

major surgeries. I've also had years when I hit the big money—then I was injured
for a year and a half. But even if I never made a nickel, I'd still stay at it.

"There are just seven blacks in rodeo, but when I started riding we had only
three. Now they have organized the American Black Rodeo Cowboy Association.
We had a parade down in Harlem that included some pretty big black stars—but
those kids back there. They'd run out just to get a touch and ask, 'Are you really a
cowboy?' Those kids wanted to see black cowboys."

I have followed the horse trailers along many a rodeo road between Tucson and
Calgary. I have sampled a fair number of the nearly 600 approved professional rodeos held annually in 42 states of the U.S.A. and four provinces of Canada. For me
each rodeo has its own special flavor. Madison Square Garden represents the West
come East. Houston's Astrodome offers the most bountiful purse. Cheyenne's
Frontier Days bursts with a Wyoming-wide vitality. Salt Lake's rodeo in the Salt
Palace seems as clean and tidy as an Ice Capades. Tucson's Fiesta de Los Vaqueros
basks in the bright Arizona sun and boasts in a Spanish accent about rodeo's origins.
The Pendleton Round-up seems as much a reunion for contesting cowboys and for
a whole teepee town of Indians. Most of all, Oklahoma City's National Finals Rodeo
crackles with competitive tensions as titans settle their championship scores.

And yet, stirring as the big rodeos may be, I remember those in smaller towns
with a particular vividness. In Paducah, Texas, after a long drought had broken, I
once watched cowboys vanish completely when broncs dumped them in a mud
wallow. And in Red Lodge, Montana—but that has a special place in rodeo.

Rodeo clown Chuck Henson first told me about Red Lodge. Chuck was playing
the Tucson rodeo and was wearing his freckle-faced, snaggle-toothed makeup; and
he got to telling about his family. "Grandpapa rode bucking horses and worked the
wild-horse race," said Chuck. "Grandpapa was called Packsaddle Ben Greenough.
Then came his kids. Uncle Frank—he's ranching now. And my uncle Turk—he was
world champion saddle-bronc rider. And my Aunt Alice Greenough—she was
the world champion lady saddle-bronc rider. Later, Mom won the same title. When
I started rodeoing, I was the only fellow that ever asked, 'Hey, Mom, how do you
think I should ride this horse?' She knew. She'd ridden the same bronc."

Chuck's mother dropped by a few minutes later—a trim, attractive woman who
looked 40 but has been married 41 years.

"Yes," said Margie Henson, "I met my husband Heavy Henson—his real name's
Charlie—when we were both rodeoing. So Chuck grew up at rodeos. While I was
riding, one of the cowboys would take care of the baby. After he got a little bigger,
he just hung on the fence. I've had one ankle broken twice and a leg and ribs and
shoulders—that all goes along with it. My legs don't match, but they work pretty
good. It's been a lot of fun. And now I do stunt work for the movies.

"Rodeo just seemed the natural thing for us Greenoughs. We came from Red
Lodge, Montana. A lot of rodeo people come from around there: the Lindermans
and the McDowell boys—are you related? We like to get back to Red Lodge on the
Fourth of July. You ought to go."

So I followed Margie Henson's advice. All of the 2,200 people of Red Lodge must have been on hand—along with thousands of outsiders for one of the really great rodeos in North America. "Some cowboys are on their way to Calgary next week," said Gene Anderson, the rodeo president. "This is our forty-second annual rodeo. And we've worked things out with Cody, Wyoming, and Livingston, Montana —the contestants can commute among the three rodeos."

At the fairgrounds, we took our seats in a grandstand below magnificent conifer-clad mountains—the Big Horns on one side, the Crazy Mountains on the other. The rodeo was a good one, with lively animals and competitive cowboys. Most of the big-name men were there. I waved to Larry Mahan, for five amazing years the world champion all-around rodeo cowboy. Larry grinned—a dazzling, ingenuous grin—and waved back. He's the man *Time* magazine called "the cowboy in the gray flannel suit." But this, his ninth year on the circuit, was giving him trouble. Young Phil Lyne, a 24-year-old from George West, Texas, was leading Larry for the title. I looked again—and there, as close to Larry as their pointed competition, stood Phil himself.

Over the public-address system the announcer intoned, "Yes, sir. At Red Lodge, you're right close to the action." We were, all afternoon. And as the events ended, we watched five private planes taxi and take off—carrying cowboys to the Livingston rodeo for the evening.

Tiny Red Lodge is not alone in producing great rodeo stars. At the national finals in Oklahoma City I asked steer wrestler Jim Poteet how he explained the success of Duncan, Oklahoma: Of the eleven Oklahomans in the finals, seven came from Duncan, population 27,000. "In Duncan," said Jim, "a cowboy is respected — the stores will even give him credit."

When I visited Duncan for myself, I found people in that modern little city very proud of their oil prosperity—"You bet, we have a lot of oil millionaires"—as well as their rodeo stars. "You know our barrel racer Missy Long?" one man asked. "A champion and just 15—still too young to get a driver's license."

"The Chisholm Trail went right past here," said Mrs. George Jenkins, president of the Stephens County Historical Society. "The trail drivers watered their herds here at Cow Creek." And there, perhaps, lies the reason rodeo grows so well here: Cowboy skills have always been part of the Duncan way of life.

Like men, like animals. And thus in Canada the men who make the Calgary Exhibition & Stampede assure their own supply of lively rodeo stock.

"You can even see where we're raising our own bucking horses," saddle-bronc champion Winston Bruce told me. We drove past Alberta's Dead Horse Lake and over the hard ice of the Red Deer River toward Hanna. There we met manager Jim Armstrong and toured a snowy sampling of the 20,000 acres where the Stampede organization runs 300 bucking horses. "That's Cindy Rocket." Jim pointed out a neat little gray mare, a bareback bucking star in her own right. "Would we sell her for $15,000 before we starved to death?" Jim laughed. "I just don't know. Now you want to see Old Red." I did. Old Red, otherwise called Red Wing, is a sorrel bronc, age 26, a champion and a favorite of all Canada. Venerable as he is, Red Wing stays out in the minus-35-degree weather, eats his fill of oats, and would be bucking soon again in Edmonton. "Yep, he stays in good shape," said Jim.

"But rodeo is inhumane!" insists a lady I know. "The animals are tortured."

Therewith she produces pamphlets printed by an organization that campaigns to stop the use of electric cattle prods, bucking straps belted around the flanks of bulls and broncs, and "barbed wire used in the mouths of the horses."

Because of her concern, and the concern of many others, I have looked carefully into such practices. I can honestly say that I've never found anyone able to document an instance of barbed wire used in a horse's mouth at any rodeo. Such a thing would be cruel indeed.

Electric prods, "hotshots," are another matter. "We have urged people to use the hotshot on the flanks and shoulders," said Milt Searle, a spokesman for The American Humane Association, oldest and largest of the humane societies. "The electric cattle prod, commonly used in moving livestock, is a lot better than a sharp object. With a 12-volt charge, the hotshot gives a jolt, not pain."

I tried a 12-volt prod on myself and found it like the jolt of an auto spark plug.

"We don't endorse rodeos," Mr. Searle continued. "But by working with rodeo people we stop a lot more cruelty than we would by opposing everything."

The organization actively discourages wild-horse racing and steer busting, an event in which the steer is roped by the horns, then tripped hard to the ground by slack rope looped around its hindquarters. "Too much risk for the animals," Mr. Searle said. "But meantime, take a look at the rules of the Rodeo Cowboys Association." For example, calves used for roping must now weigh at least 200 pounds.

But what about the bucking strap?

"Horses are just ticklish," Casey Tibbs told me. "When I was a boy we would put our heels in a horse's flanks so he'd blow up and buck. Like hitting a kneecap. My sisters used to tickle me the same way. A flank strap works like that. And remember, by R.C.A. rules the straps have to be fleece-lined. The only thing inhumane about a flank strap is you have to kill the sheep to line the strap."

Rodeo producer John Snow made another point. "If a horse is mistreated and hurt he'll quit bucking—to escape pain—and simply become cowed and docile. Now if the flank strap did cause the horse excruciating pain, the horse would stop, and we'd have pretty dull rodeos, wouldn't we?"

"A bucking horse represents a hefty investment," rodeo stock producer Tommy Steiner told me. "And most producers protect that investment. The horses often live to great age, still bucking at rodeos, and not ground up into dogfood."

Many of rodeo's critics, of course, argue convincingly for their point of view. Oddly, however, most of them have said little about calf roping. The men who know the cattle arts best are the ones who raise objections here.

Amarillo brand inspector and former Pitchfork cowboy Red Bennett put it this way: "I feel sorry for those little calves—steers too. I like for everything to have a real fighting chance—and they don't have it." Coming from Red, who in line of duty may rope two dozen head of cattle every day, that objection is convincing indeed.

Still, The American Humane Association reports the animal injury rate sharply down—to only one-tenth of one percent, or "approximately the same as for animals on the ranch." For my own part, I have seen far more cowboys hurt than rodeo animals.

One Colorado rancher with an assembly-line view of the cattle business told me he still feels that rodeo has an enduring place in America. "That's the place for roping," he said, "and all the other old ways."

And one venerable Texan I know declared firmly, "The old ways are going—on all the ranches—and good riddance."

"No," insisted Blaine Sidwell, of that unbelievably huge cattle spread, the four-million-acre Gang Ranch in British Columbia. "No, the old ways won't change here—the country is too big to change."

Then Blaine and his kinfolk supported their claim by showing me a grassy document more than five times the size of Rhode Island. Some 18 Sidwells run the ranch under a partnership arrangement. Redheaded Bill Sidwell, age 19, took me up Table Mountain for an astronaut's view of the Fraser River country and its gulleys and mountains, its bunch-grass meadows and its forests of fir and jackpine.

"It's a long ways back in there," Bill told me. He spent his first summer in a cow camp at age 15. "That was at Relay Camp. You go 34 miles by four-wheel drive, then take packhorses and go up another 30 miles. Takes days. But in an emergency, you can make it down in 12 hours, changing horses at the other camps."

Names of the other cow camps sound like early Zane Grey: Hungry Valley, Lost Valley, Graveyard, and so on.

Charlie Hance, a 71-year-old Indian of Chilcotin and Shuswap blood, helped name Hungry Valley in the 1920's when he drove the first cows up there. "We ran out of grub," he explained, "and had to butcher a calf a day."

Lost Valley got its name from an old prospector. "About 1934 he disappeared there," Charlie recalled. "They finally figured a bear killed him and buried him."

"My little brother Carl—he's 15—got his first grizzly bear this summer," said Bill.

"It weighed 900 pounds," added his father Ervin Sidwell. "We called it our $50,000 grizzly, since it had probably cost us at least that much by killing two beeves a week. Figure it out. We lose at least 250 cows a year to grizzly bears alone."

Over coffee in the cookhouse the Sidwells told an evening's worth of stories about bears—wild, convincing tales: how a treed black bear caught the rocks being thrown at him and tossed them back...how Gary Sidwell roped the bear...and how Bill, armed with only a fire extinguisher, once faced an angry mother black bear; he squirted the chemicals into the bear's face at 20 feet.

"All my boys are mountain men," said Ervin Sidwell proudly. But always the talk returns to cattle. The Gang Ranch brand—JH—honors Jerome Harper, who came here from Harpers Ferry, West Virginia, with his brother in 1863 and built up a herd of 10,000 cattle. Gangs of Chinese came to dig irrigation ditches, and hay growers initiated the use of the gang plow—and thus, for one reason or another, the vast spread took the name Gang Ranch.

PAINTING BY FREDERIC REMINGTON, 1895. REMINGTON ART MUSEUM, OGDENSBURG, NEW YORK

The Sidwells have introduced modern touches—a school for 23 ranch young-sters, a generator that even powers street lights at the headquarters, and Saturday night movies for all hands. But they take greater pride in the old traditions. "We still use log fences back in the trees," said Bill. "They hold up even if a tree falls on them. Of course," he adds patronizingly, "barbed wire is all right in open country."

"And cowboys," said Ervin, "are more in demand here now than ever before."

"But some leave us," said Blaine, "because the country's too big for them."

Then they told about three rustlers they caught last summer. "Followed a trail of blood," said Ervin. "They'd butchered a cow and calf and had put the meat in their pickup. But everytime they went uphill, blood ran out.

"We told the Royal Canadian Mounted Police, so we had two Mounties with us when we found their camp. Gary and I had our rifles, and the Mounties drew their pistols. Really surprised those men. No, no trouble."

So cowboys still enjoy a wild sort of excitement. But I wonder if they can match the goings-on around Motley County, Texas, in 1893.

"Some of the old Matador Ranch hands wanted to kill me," my grandfather told me. "They figured the county government would fold up if the paper work stopped —and I did all the paper work.

"Well, one day I got an anonymous note that said, 'If you want to be carried out feet foremost, come to the dance in the Dickens schoolhouse.'

"I didn't like the sound of it—but I couldn't let them bluff me, so I went. Just to show how brave I was, I took off my pistols, threw the belt over a rail, and then sat down and played the piano." Grandfather stopped to puff on his pipe.

"Was there any shooting?" I asked.

"Nope. Not a bit. The note was probably just a joke. But it was still a good thing I went to that dance ... You see, that was the night I met a girl named Callie Jones."

They were married on December 1, 1893. And though Callie put an end to Caswell McDowell's cowboying, no grandson can rightly complain.

Index

Illustrations and illustrations references appear in *italics*.

Cattle Trails of the Old West

Millions of Longhorns—destined for eastern markets—tramped out of Texas in the 20 years after the Civil War, bound for railheads in Missouri and Kansas and grasslands farther north; other breeds moved east along such routes as the Oregon Trail. As the railroads reached Texas, the long drives came to an end.

MAP BY RICHARD SCHLECHT AND GEOGRAPHIC ART;
DRAWING BELOW BY JOE DE YONG, FROM "THE COWBOY AND
HIS INTERPRETERS," BY DOUGLAS BRANCH, 1926

Additional Reading

E. C. ("Teddy Blue") Abbott and Helena Huntington Smith, *We Pointed Them North;* Andy Adams, *The Log of a Cowboy;* Ramon F. Adams, ed., *The Best of the American Cowboy; The Old-Time Cowhand;* Ramon F. Adams and Homer E. Britzman, *Charles M. Russell: The Cowboy Artist;* Douglas Branch, *The Cowboy and His Interpreters;* Mark H. Brown and W. R. Felton, *Before Barbed Wire; The Frontier Years;* Edward Everett Dale, *Cow Country; The Range Cattle Industry;* J. Frank Dobie, *The Longhorns.*

Harry Sinclair Drago, *Great American Cattle Trails; The Great Range Wars; Red River Valley; Wild, Woolly & Wicked;* Cordelia Sloan Duke and Joe B. Frantz, *6,000 Miles of Fence: Life on the XIT Ranch of Texas;* Richard Dunlop, *Great Trails of the West;* Philip Durham and Everett L. Jones, *The Negro Cowboys;* George N. Fenin and William K. Everson, *The Western;* Robert H. Fletcher, *Free Grass to Fences;* Joe B. Frantz and Julian Ernest Choate, Jr., *The American Cowboy: The Myth and The Reality.*

Wayne Gard, *The Chisholm Trail; Reminiscences of Range Life;* Fred Gipson, *Fabulous Empire, Colonel Zack Miller's Story;* Ben K. Green, *Back to Back;* Zane Grey, *Riders of the Purple Sage;* Herman Hagedorn, *Roosevelt in the Badlands;* J. Evetts Haley, *Fort Concho and The Texas Frontier; Charles Goodnight, Cowman and Plainsman; The XIT Ranch of Texas and the Early Days of the Llano Estacado;* William Loren Katz, *The Black West;* Joseph G. McCoy, *Historic Sketches of the Cattle Trade of the West and Southwest;* Louis Pelzer, *The Cattlemen's Frontier;* M. S. Robertson, *Rodeo.*

Theodore Roosevelt, *Ranch Life and the Hunting Trail;* Joseph G. Rosa, *They Called Him Wild Bill;* Don Russell, *The Lives and Legends of Buffalo Bill; The Wild West;* Mari Sandoz, *The Cattlemen;* Charles A. Siringo, *A Texas Cowboy or Fifteen Years on the Hurricane Deck of a Spanish Pony;* Charles L. Sonnichsen, *Cowboys and Cattle Kings;* Kent Ladd Steckmesser, *The Western Hero in History and Legend;* Floyd B. Streeter, *Prairie Trails and Cow Towns;* Charles Wayland Towne and Edward Norris Wentworth, *Cattle and Men;* Walter Prescott Webb, *The Great Plains;* The Walter Prescott Webb Memorial Lectures, *Essays on the American West;* Paul J. Wellman, *The Trampling Herd;* Owen Wister, *The Virginian;* Robert M. Wright, *Dodge City, The Cowboy Capital.*

Composition for *The American Cowboy* by National Geographic's Phototypographic Division, John E. McConnell, Manager. Printed and bound by Fawcett Printing Corp., Rockville, Md. Color separations by Graphic Color Plate, Inc., Stamford, Conn.; The Lanman Company, Alexandria, Va.; Progressive Color Corp., Rockville, Md.